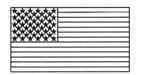   

BRIDGES

A Self-Esteem Activity Book
for Students in Grades 4-6

J. Victor McGuire
Sonoma State University
Rohnert Park, CA

Bobbi Heuss
Timberview Middle School
Colorado Springs, CO

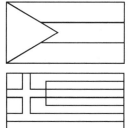

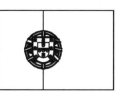

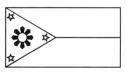

Illustrations by
Karla Kay Asplin

Allyn and Bacon
Boston □ London □ Toronto □ Sydney □ Tokyo □ Singapore

Copyright © 1995 by Allyn & Bacon
A Simon & Schuster Company
Needham Heights, Mass. 02194

Library of Congress Cataloging-in-Publication Data

McGuire, J.Victor

    Bridges: a self-esteem activity book for students in grades 4-6 / by J. Victor McGuire, Bobbi Heuss; Illustrations by Karla Kay Asplin.

    p. cm.

    ISBN 0-205-16504-4:

    1. School children — United States — Psychology — Handbooks, manuals, etc. 2. Self-esteem in children — United States — Handbooks, manuals, etc. 3. Education, Elementary — Activity programs — United States - Handbooks, manuals, etc. I. Heuss, Bobbi. II. Title.

LB1117.M34 1994

372.18'1—dc20
                                              94-30011
                                                CIP

Printed in the United States of America
10 9 8 7 6 5 4 3 2 1   99 98 97 96 95 94

One evening when our daughter Jennifer was in the third grade and industriously investigating the dictionary, we had a marvelous conversation about words and dictionaries.

We proceeded to look up the word 'today,' then went to 'yesterday,' and finally we went looking for, as Jennifer quite naturally explained, 'tomorrowday.'

"But Daddy, why isn't there a word 'tomorrowday?' 'Today' and 'yesterday' both have the word 'day' in them; there should be a 'day' in 'tomorrow!' " We both laughed at the possibility that Jennifer had invented a new word, and our excitement increased as we planned to submit "the newest word in the English language" to the dictionary people.

To this day, Jennifer and I refer to 'tomorrowday' with a warm sense of personal pride in having invented our new word, and I am continuously reminded by this example of the depth of creativity and fresh perspective inherent in our young people. Our daily lives are, of course, filled with magical moments like this example, but it seems, at times, that we are less aware, or possibly less appreciative, of them as we get caught up with the seemingly larger challenges we all face in our homes, schools and communities.

It seems to me that a most serious challenge we all face is to somehow maintain the creativity and fresh perspective of youth as we grow in experience, knowing that the curiosity and competence to be more effective human beings is the real bottom line, regardless of the undertaking. Whether we are engaged in a formal strategy such as BRIDGES or a more casual investigation of words in a dictionary, it is critical that we take time to appreciate the sensitivity, the undaunted enthusiasm, and the unqualified love of our young people, for we all have potential to be "young people," regardless of our age.

Self-esteem development is a lifelong process that requires constant attention, and each person needs to develop a strategy for internalizing its importance. I am reminded of a good friend's admonition to me several years ago when I was just beginning my teaching career; in a sentence, he captured my belief system about leadership development: **"The most important ideas people have are those ideas they have about themselves."** That's still a good reminder for me today, and I expect it will be equally as valuable tomorrowday!

Dr. Tom Giblin
Superintendent of Schools
Gilford, Connecticut

Children Learn What They Live

If children live with criticism, they learn to condemn.

If children live with hostility, they learn to fight.

If children live with ridicule, they learn to be shy.

If children live with shame, they learn to feel guilty.

If children live with tolerance, they learn to be patient.

If children live with encouragement, they learn confidence.

If children live with praise, they learn to appreciate.

If children live with fairness, they learn justice.

If children live with security, they learn to have faith.

If children live with approval, they learn to like themselves.

If children live with acceptance and friendship,

    they learn to find love in the world.

Author Unknown

CONTENTS

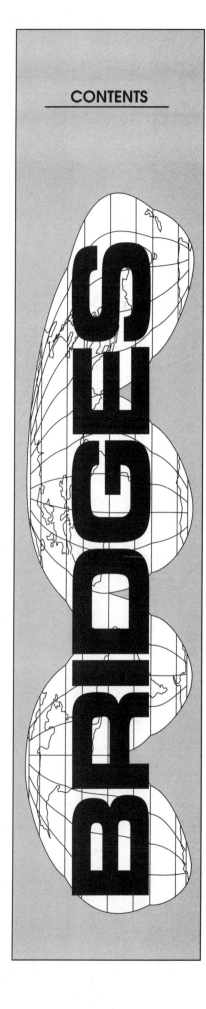

CONTENTS

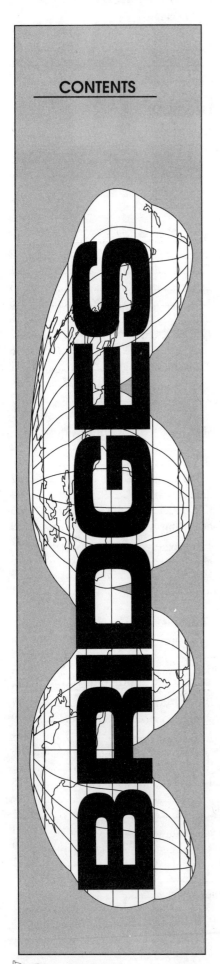

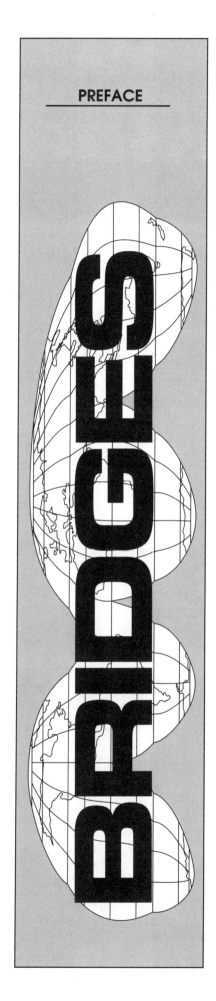

*A*s I travel across the country addressing audiences on self-esteem, motivation and communication issues, inevitably comments are made sounding like, "What can be done for our elementary students?" and "We need to impact children early, before it's too late."

I encountered those statements time and time again until I decided, with the help of others, to create a comprehensive elementary program that would focus on four main areas: SENSITIVITY, SELF-ESTEEM, COMMUNICATION and MOTIVATION. My desire was to do this with a curriculum to be utilized by teachers, parents, counselors, youth group coordinators, and anyone who wanted to work in a non-threatening and interactive environment with elementary children.

Therefore, **Bridges** was created.

Ideally, each instructor would have his/her own manual of the **Bridges** program to be used for one class. Use it to take notes, jot down new ideas, and modify it to the specific needs of your students. Make it yours.

Student pages are available to copy.

J. Victor McGuire, Ph.D.
Founder, Spice of Life Educational Opportunities
Co-Author of *Bridges*

Acknowledgements

Over the last five years many people have supported my efforts in an assortment of ways. I truly appreciate their patience and understanding during this period. They are all wonderful. Thanks!

Dr. Jane McDearmid
Dr. Timothy Houlton
Ms. Dee Wanger
Mr. Bill Grunewald
Ms. Margot Collins
Dr. Rich Feller
Mr. Wayne Parthan
Ms. Josette Dillman
Ms. Bobbi Heuss
Ms. Caryl Thomason
Dr. H. Mack Clark
Mr. Louis & Ellen McGuire
Ms. Sally Hutchinson
Ms. Karla Kay Asplin

 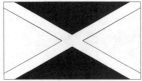  

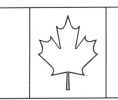

P A R T • O N E

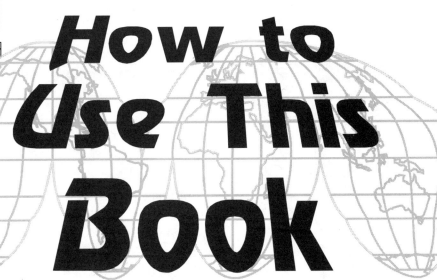

How to Use This Book

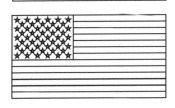
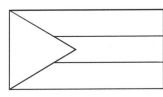

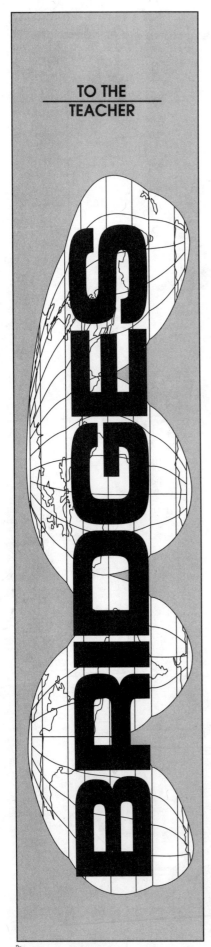

 ridges is a self-esteem program created by **Spice of Life Educational Opportunities**. It was designed for students in grades four, five and six and centers around four main areas:

- **Sensitivity**

- **Self-Esteem**

- **Communication**

- **Motivation**

The primary factor in determining whether this program will succeed is <u>YOU</u>, the teacher/facilitator. YOU will be the one who sets the tone for the sessions, and YOU will be the role model who demonstrates what the real meaning and value of the program is. YOU will be following up on the goals of the program and making sure that students are moving forward. It's a big job, but it's well worth your time and effort!

Here are some suggestions to keep in mind:

- Approach each session with a very positive attitude.

- Make each session relaxed and enjoyable for all.

- Let students know the objective of each session.

- Be certain that all students are participating.

- Always look for examples of behavior that illustrate any objectives and point them out to the class.

- Encourage students to make the objectives part of their daily lives.

- Convey a sense of importance about the objectives to the students.

NOTE: *The use of gender throughout this book has been simplified to either he or she in many cases for easier readability. It is not intended to be specific to one gender only.*

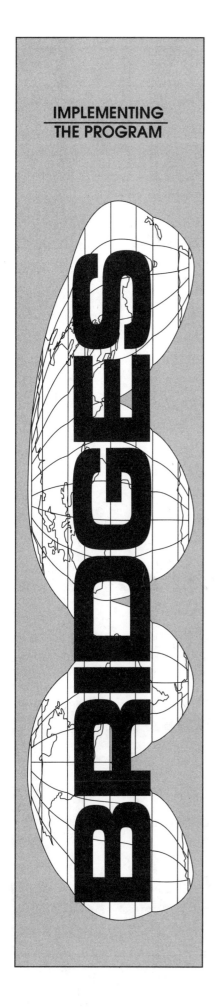

How Bridges Works

There are 50 sessions in the **Bridges** program. Some of the sessions may require more than one class meeting time. And, as you would in regular classroom activities, it is important that students are encouraged to participate.

It's possible to set up your **Bridges** program in any number of ways:

A. **One Semester** — Regular class meetings about a half hour long, 2-3 times a week.

B. **Year Long** — Regular class meetings about a half hour long, 1-2 times a week.

C. **Customized** — Intensive at first, with follow-up throughout the year. Introduce each chapter, choose activities to emphasize the main points, then use the other activities when needed throughout the year.

D. **Student Pages** — Copy the student pages for your class. This will save your school money on the purchasing of student booklets because you will use specifically the pages and quantity you need. When you find the symbol "❏" located by the page number, it denotes a page to be copied.

NOTE: *It is not recommended that you try to cover all the material in less than one semester.*

I try to learn as much as I can because I know nothing compared to what I need to know.

Muhammad Ali

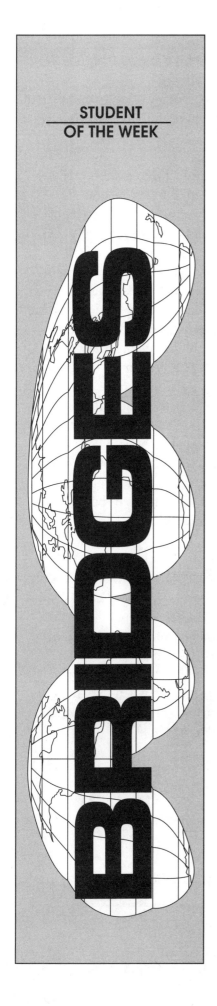

Everyone wants to feel important. Have either the teacher or the students select a "Student of the Week." This can be done either on a volunteer basis or randomly making sure that each student gets an opportunity to be the "Student of the Week."

Bridges suggests you set up a special bulletin board or display area which the "Student of the Week" can use to create a display showing what he/she collects, favorite books or hobbies, awards received, photographs of places lived or visited, recent and baby pictures . . . anything that lets his classmates know more about him/her.

Set up a regular schedule for taking down (and putting up) the student's display, i.e. put up on Monday mornings, take down on Friday afternoons.

You may also choose to give the "Student of the Week" some special privileges such as sitting wherever he/she wishes for the week, being line leader and/or messenger, having lunch with the teacher, etc.

Sometime during the week, ask the students to write special, positive notes to the "Student of the Week" telling what they like about him/her. These may be written on "sticky" notes and put on display or simply given to the student.

At the end of the week the class should tell something new they learned about the "Student of the Week."

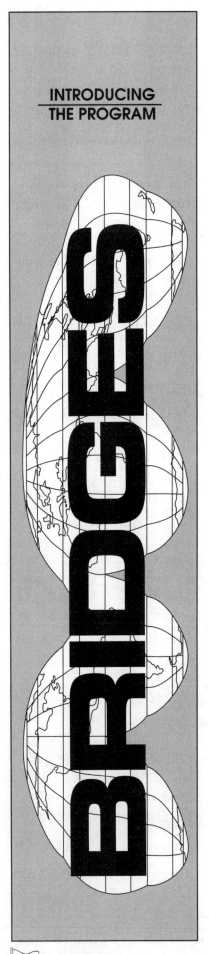

Introduce the program by saying that the entire class is going to participate in the **Bridges** program, developed by Spice of Life Educational Opportunities. Ask them what they think the program is about based on its name.

After students have given their ideas, have them read the introduction in their books together to learn about the program. Elaborate on the introduction by telling them that **Bridges** is a leadership program developed to help students get to know themselves and others better. It focuses on the POSITIVE and will give them new "tools" for handling the challenges and problems of everyday life. It will help all of us begin to understand where people are "coming from," what they are saying, what they mean, what they want and why they are doing what they are doing. The program will help us all become better people.

At this point, give the class details about how the program will work in your class, including the rules you have set up for discussions, when the class will meet, and how it will be divided, if at all. In addition, tell them that this program is not graded but you do expect a personal commitment from each student. Discuss the advantages of being an active participant in the program.

To demonstrate how little the students know each other, start with this brief activity: Ask questions like: "Who knows what Mary's favorite food is?", "What kind of sport does Sam like best?", "Does Mike have a pet?", "What kind?", "Who in this room comes from the largest family?" . . . "the smallest family?" etc.

When this is finished, tell the students when they're going to meet again for their session. Be sure to emphasize that you're really looking forward to it!

Any thoughts?
Put them here!

Tact is
the ability to close
your mouth
before someone else
wants to.

Anonymous

P A R T • T W O

SENSITIVITY

Helping students better

understand the concept

of sensitivity

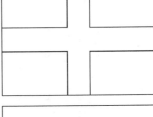

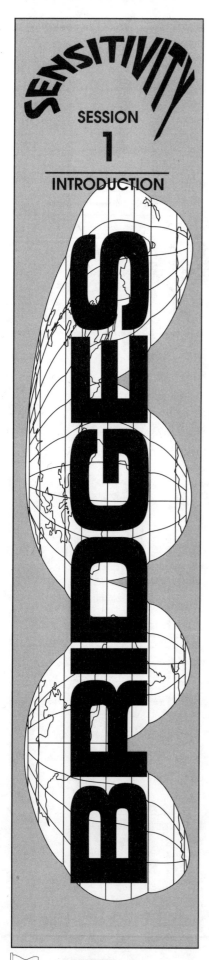

Much of this introductory lesson is designed to make students aware of exactly what sensitivity is. Spend some time reading the introduction to the chapter with the students. See if they can come up with other examples, preferably involving other students who have shown sensitivity.

Be sure to emphasize the difference between being sensitive and being overly sensitive. Sensitivity as used in this chapter is a positive quality and includes caring about others and showing empathy. It is outward-directed and unselfish. Overly sensitive people, on the other hand, react in an inward manner to what others say to and about them. They are quick to take offense and are certain that other people are always talking about them. It is usually a very insecure person who is overly sensitive.

Following this discussion have students fill out page 14. You will want to take a few minutes afterwards to have students read their responses. That way students may add to their books after listening to others.

At the end of the session, direct students' attention to the TO DO section at the bottom of the page. Tell them the date of the next session so they will be certain to have their items in class by that time. Discuss briefly what kinds of things they might bring.

Examples:
- an old stuffed animal they've had for years
- a photo of their grandparents who live in a different city
- an article that describes the plight of migrant workers
- a token gift that a friend gave them before they moved
- a picture of a puppy or kitten
- a souvenir of a special day that involved sensitivity
- a card or letter they've saved because of its meaning or because it's a reminder of a special person

Be sure that you also bring in something for the discussion.

A friend is a present you give yourself.

Robert Louis Stevenson

Welcome to

BRIDGES

You are about to begin a program that is designed for you. You are important and special. There is no one else on earth who has your qualities and personality. Isn't it nice to know that you are unique?

Bridges from Spice of Life Educational Opportunities is meant to help you discover how very special you are. As with most things in life, the more you put into this, the more you will get out of it. With **Bridges**, however, you are going to learn about your classmates as well as yourself. You'll find that you are the same as others your age in many ways . . . and different from them in many other respects. Doesn't that sound great?

C'mon now... let's begin!

SENSITIVITY

Have you ever felt happy because you saw that someone else felt that way, and you shared their joy?

Have you ever seen a picture that made you feel happy or sad?

Have you ever felt sort of blue because you knew that something sad had happened to someone else?

Is there something in your home that gives you a special feeling whenever you see or think about it?

If so, you have shown **SENSITIVITY** . . . and that's good!

You probably learned some of your sensitivity from experiencing it yourself. An example is when someone cheered you up when you were feeling down. Maybe they talked to you about your problem, or perhaps they simply put their arm around your shoulder. Regardless of what they did, you got the idea that they cared. You probably wanted to be around that person whenever you could because they were so sensitive to your needs, right?

Would you like to have people think of you as a sensitive person? You probably would because you know how important it is. Being sensitive will help you get along with others. That's what this chapter is all about!

BOP ON!

Please answer the following questions:

1. When you think about sensitivity, how do you **define** it? *(You may use examples to illustrate what you mean.)*

_____

_____

_____

_____

_____

2. What are some other words that **describe** people who are sensitive? How do they act?

_____

_____

_____

_____

TO DO:

Bring in something for the next class session that brings out the sensitivity in you. It may be a picture, a magazine or newspaper clipping, a special article from home or anything else you find suitable. We'll share these items in class.

Answer Page

Please answer the following questions:

1. When you think about sensitivity, how do you **define** it? *(You may use examples to illustrate what you mean.)*

When you're finished with the discussion, students should have the ideas of such things as: awareness, feelings,

empathy, perception, responsiveness, reaction, thoughtfulness, sentimentality, affection, intuition, appreciation,

inclination to action, emotion, sensibility. Be certain that students understand the difference between being sensitive

as it is meant here, and being "too sensitive," meaning quick to take offense.

2. What are some other words that **describe** people who are sensitive? How do they act?

Kind, considerate, caring, thoughtful, nice, friendly, compassionate, affectionate, etc.

Bring in something for the next class session that brings out the sensitivity in you. It may be a picture, a magazine or newspaper clipping, a special article from home or anything else you find suitable. We'll share these items in class.

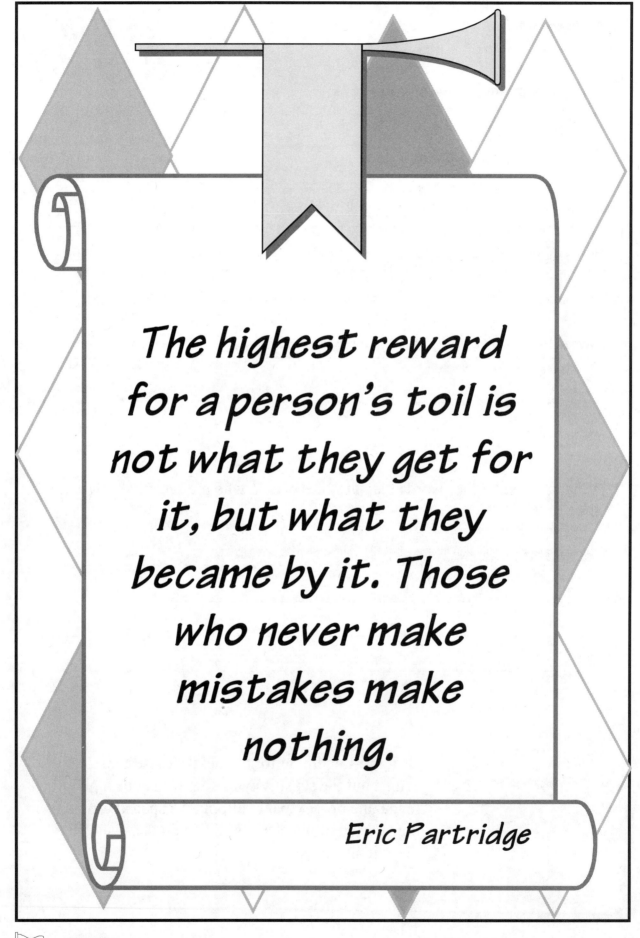

The highest reward for a person's toil is not what they get for it, but what they became by it. Those who never make mistakes make nothing.

Eric Partridge

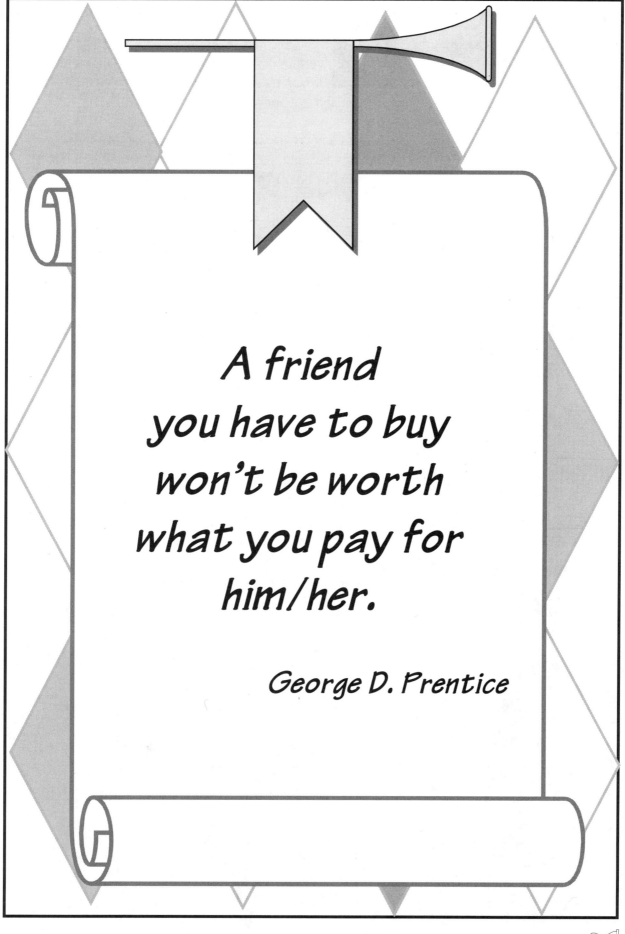

A friend
you have to buy
won't be worth
what you pay for
him/her.

George D. Prentice

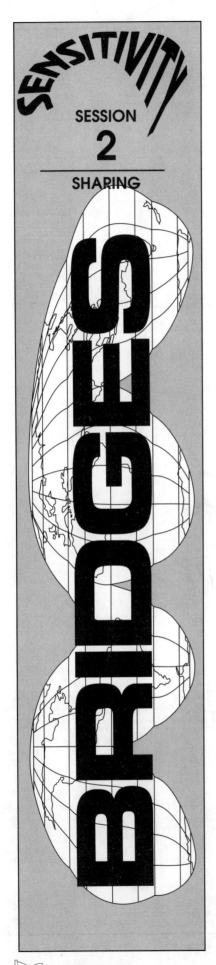

SENSITIVITY

SESSION

2

SHARING

BRIDGES

Start this session by reviewing the definition and qualities of a sensitive person. When you're certain that all students understand it, begin the lesson by sharing the item you brought in. Tell why you chose it and what it means to you.

Have students share their items from home. In some cases, what they brought may be very personal and will not affect others in the class in any way. However, it is important to emphasize that their reactions to each other at this time should reflect sensitivity and respect.

Some students will have brought in things that may affect others. Examples might be pictures or articles from magazines. Involve the class in a discussion of these after their items have been presented.

- How does this picture make you feel?

- What do you think happened?

- What could happen to make the person in the picture feel better?

- How could the situation in the picture have been avoided?

- How does the situation in the picture make you feel?

- How do you act when you feel that way?

Please answer the following questions:

1. Describe what you brought in to share.

_____

_____

_____

2. Where did you get this item?

_____

_____

2. What does this have to do with sensitivity?

_____

_____

_____

A person who is
his/her own doctor
has a fool
for a patient.

American Proverb

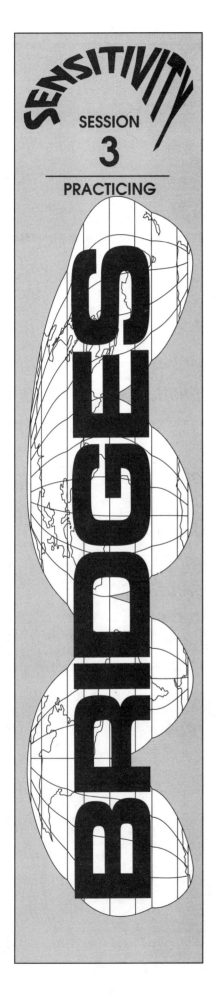

 tudents will be doing a creative writing assignment in Session 3, so this lesson will correlate with your language arts.

Get students prepared for writing by asking these questions:

1. Have you ever seen a TV show or read a book that really involved you emotionally? What was it that made you feel that way?

2. Have you ever witnessed a situation that made you really feel a part of it, even though you weren't? Perhaps you felt really good for an athlete who won at the Olympics . . . or perhaps you felt very bad about an accident.

3. Have you ever imagined yourself in a situation where you experienced sensitivity toward what was happening to someone else? Perhaps you heard of someone who was hurting and you thought of what you might say or do to help.

Tell students that you're going to give them some time to write a story about a situation that involves sensitivity. They should tell what happened and how they felt about it. As with all good stories, it should have a beginning, middle and end. The development of the problem and the part that sensitivity plays in its solution will be the bulk of the story.

Emphasize that these stories will not be graded, but they will be collected, and some of them will be read aloud to the class anonymously. The due date on the stories should be the next **Bridges** class session.

WINNER vs. LOSER

The Winner is always part of the answer;
The Loser is always part of the problem.
The Winner always has a program;
The Loser always has an excuse.
The Winner says "Let me do it for you;"
The Loser says "That's not my job."
The Winner sees an answer for every problem;
The Loser sees a problem for every answer.
The Winner sees a green near every sand trap;
The Loser sees 2-3 sand traps near every
   green.
The Winner says "It may be difficult, but it's
possible;
The Loser says "It may be possible, but it's
too difficult.

Be a Winner!

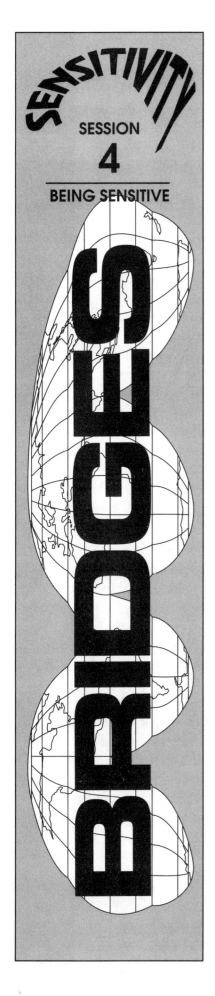

ollect stories from the last session before beginning today's activity. That will allow you time before the next session to go over the stories and select the ones you wish to use.

Goal: By working together in a group, students may learn to be more sensitive to each other's needs.

Preparation/Notes: Using tagboard, the teacher cuts out puzzle shapes from an 8" x 8" square, making twice as many pieces as there will be students in each group. The puzzle shapes should have straight sides. (It is advised that you duplicate the same puzzle for each group to ensure equality of difficulty.) When the groups are formed, the teacher should give each student two pieces of the puzzle that his/her group needs.

Do not use a picture puzzle for this. One of the advantages of plain tagboard is that it looks the same on both sides. Students will learn by watching each other that the pieces can sometimes be turned over to fit correctly.

Construction paper may also be used, but it is a little more difficult to work with since it is not as heavy as tagboard. However, it does have the advantage of coming in colors that enable you to keep the different groups' pieces separated.

With a very small number of students, it may be preferable to have only one piece per person.

Procedure: Students will be divided into groups of 5-6 each. Students are instructed to put the puzzle together as quickly and efficiently as possible, keeping these rules in mind:

1. They may not speak to each other.
2. They may not gesture to each other or point to the pieces of the puzzle.
3. Students may give pieces of the puzzle to others, but they may not take pieces from anyone. They may not give all their pieces away; they may exchange pieces.
4. The group may not put all the pieces into one pile in the center of the table. Individuals who choose to must give their puzzle pieces directly to someone else.
5. The group should work together on the puzzle. Their goal is to complete the puzzle while making everyone feel included and accepted.

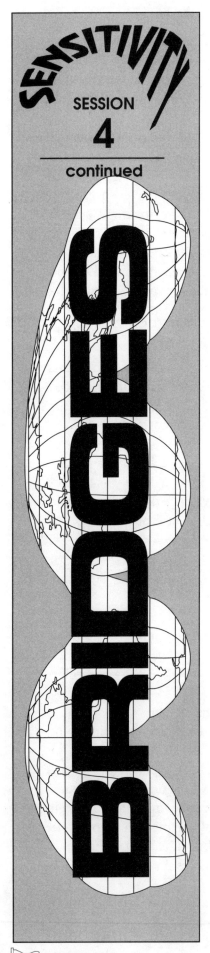
A follow-up discussion is necessary to evaluate how students accomplished both of their goals: completing the puzzle and being sensitive to including everyone in the activity. Questions should include:

- Did everyone have a part? (The parts may not have been equal, but no one should have felt left out. Perhaps the group recognized one individual's strength and gave him the lion's share to do. However, everyone should have felt they had a part in the group's decisions instead of one person dominating.)
- Did everyone seem to "tune in" to what the others were thinking? How do you know?
- Did anyone seem to be more sensitive than others? How do you know?
- What factors do you think contributed most to your group successfully completing the puzzle? If you were not successful, why?
- Is there one goal that seemed more important to your group than the another? What did the group do to make you think that?

VARIATIONS:

1. Give students a bag of objects. Ask them to create a useful object using everything in the bag. In this case they may talk, but one of the rules is that each person must place the object he/she pulled out of the bag onto the invention.

2. Blindfold every student except one in the group. Put the pieces of a very simple puzzle (such as a preschooler might work) in a bag. Have the students in the group gather around a table and empty the puzzle pieces onto the table. The unblindfolded student must communicate where the others need to put their pieces. He/She should be certain to include all the members of the group.

Note: *This activity is also good for the Communication section.*

*Treat all people
as though they
were related
to you.*

Navajo Nations

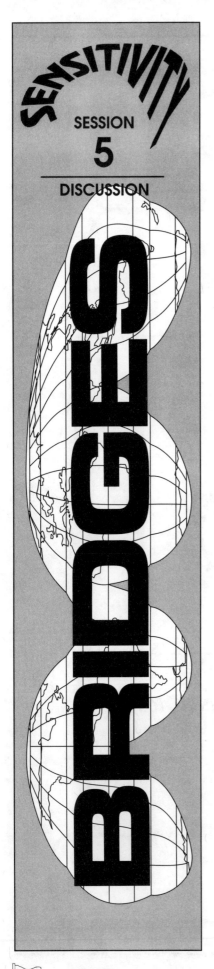

SENSITIVITY

SESSION
5

DISCUSSION

BRIDGES

Students turned in their stories during the last **Bridges** class session. Between that session and this one the teacher should have read over the stories and chosen the ones to be read aloud in class. The names of the authors should not be told. If the group has been divided in two, the teacher may want to read stories from one half to the other half.

Students should discuss the feelings involved in the stories and how sensitivity played a part. If there's time they may want to invent other endings that could evolve from a lack of sensitivity and then compare the two story versions.

Behold the turtle;
It makes progress
only when it
sticks its
neck out.

James Bryant Conant

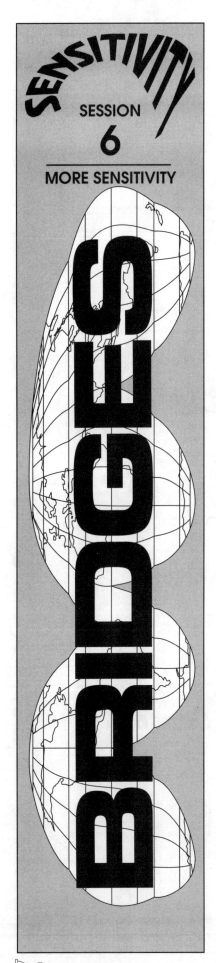

SENSITIVITY

SESSION

6

MORE SENSITIVITY

BRIDGES

his session will actually give students a chance to practice being sensitive through role playing. Nine separate situations are suggested on the following pages. You can use these or make up your own.

Go over the following rules with the students for this activity:

1. Stay in your role. Make your character realistic.

2. Remember that your objective is to be sensitive to others. There may be things you could say that would solve the problem; however, if you don't show respect for others' feelings, it's not acceptable.

3. Recognize that there may be more than one way to effectively handle a situation. Try each one several times, varying the way the situation is handled.

4. Be respectful as a member of the audience. Be sensitive to the way the actors are feeling.

After each situation is role played, follow-up with a brief discussion. See if the students feel that the actors' portrayals were realistic and sensitive.

Practicing SENSITIVITY

In order to be really sensitive, we should follow the Golden Rule:

Treat Others As You Want To Be Treated.

Think about it. You can act most sensitively if you mentally put yourself in the other person's place and imagine how he must feel. This means you don't just look at other people on the surface, but you also try to figure out how they are feeling inside. Once you can do that, you can act accordingly.

Try your hand at role playing these situations. In each case try to be really sensitive in how you act and what you say.

A friend of yours has just flunked a test that she really studied for and she is depressed. What do you say to her? How do you act?

There is a person that you do not particularly like, and he/she follows you and your best friend around all the time. You think it's important to be friendly, but this situation is really getting on your nerves. What can you say to this person? What do you say to your best friend, who wants you to get rid of the other person? How do you act?

Your two best friends are angry with each other, and both of them are trying to get you to be on their side in the argument. They both insist that the other one is spreading rumors about them. How do you behave toward them? What do you say?

Practicing SENSITIVITY

Your best friend is becoming good friends with someone else, and you feel that you are being left out of their fun. How do you handle this situation?

A friend of yours had a pet dog that died and he/she is feeling absolutely awful about it. What do you do? What do you say?

You just won a writing contest, and you're very happy about it. The judges were particularly impressed with the originality of the idea in the writing. You know that the winning idea was not yours, although you did the actual writing. The person who gave you the idea did not win anything in the contest and he/she is very upset. What do you do? What do you say?

You have a lot of friends, and you really enjoy being with them. You notice another student sitting alone each lunch period. You don't know if this person likes eating alone or if he would like to be with someone. One thing's for certain—he is too shy to join your group, and you would like to be with them. What do you do? What do you say?

Someone with whom you'd like to be friends asks if she can copy your homework because she didn't get an assignment done. What do you say?

There's a student on your volleyball team who is obnoxious. He is always trying to be the center of attention. He doesn't have any friends, and you feel reasonably certain that the way he acts is the reason. Whenever you try to be friendly to him, your friends make fun of you which bothers you very much. What do you do or say to the person who is obnoxious. What do you do or say to your friends?

TO DO:

Make up some situations of your own and have members of the class role play them, too!

*You don't have to
teach people
to be human.
You have to teach
them how to stop
being inhuman.*

Eldridge Cleaver

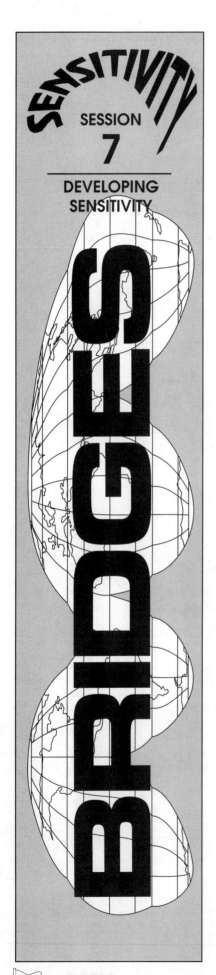

t is hoped that by this time students will have learned to recognize sensitive behavior and its importance. Session 18 gives them the responsibility of developing that behavior in themselves.

The following page gives suggestions regarding where sensitivity can be developed. Go over each of them with the class. Discuss why each might be an important situation for showing sensitivity.

If possible take a half-day field trip to a nursing home or institution for the deaf, blind and/or retarded to introduce this lesson. This would lead to some very meaningful discussion.

It's important that students realize that sensitivity is an ongoing goal. Sometimes it's easier to be sensitive toward the people who are not around us everyday and/or are less fortunate. A one-time visit to a nursing home may help increase awareness, but it may not do much on a daily basis. If students always try to be sensitive it will make a bigger difference in their lives and the lives of the people they know than if they show sensitivity through activities designed to be done only periodically.

For this session students should choose to observe someone in one of the situations described or make up one of their own. When they do or say something they feel is really sensitive, they should record it on the page and be prepared to share it with the class during the next session.

DEVELOPING
SENSITIVITY

Sometimes people learn to be more sensitive by really concentrating on it. Take a day to watch another person and try to put yourself in his/her place. Use the suggestions below or think of your own. See how it "feels" to be that person. Then think to yourself , "How would I want to be treated if I were him/her?"

- At home, watch someone else in your family. Try to see him in a different light. Pay attention to how that person contributes to the family. Be sensitive to how he is feeling. Do something for him. Let him know they are important to you.

  Make a point of looking around for ways of helping other people.

- Visit a neighbor. Try to find something to do or say that will make her feel great!

- Look around your school for someone who seems to be feeling left out. Start a conversation with him or include him in something you are doing.

  You can make a positive difference in the lives of others.

- If you babysit, give your undivided attention to the child(ren) and see if you can make them feel very special.

- Make a point of being very friendly to the clerk who is waiting on you in a store or the serviceman who has come to work at your home.

- Visit and help in a kindergarten class or a handicapped class at your school. See how much you can be a help to the teacher.

- Spend some time with your school cooks, custodians, or other support staff to see what their jobs are like. Become more sensitive to them as part of your school community.

  The world will be a better place simply because you care.

DEVELOPING

SENSITIVITY

What I did: _____

_____

_____

_____

What I saw and learned:

_____

_____

_____

_____

How this experience helped me become more sensitive:

_____

_____

_____

_____

_____

_____

Be sure to share your experiences with the group!

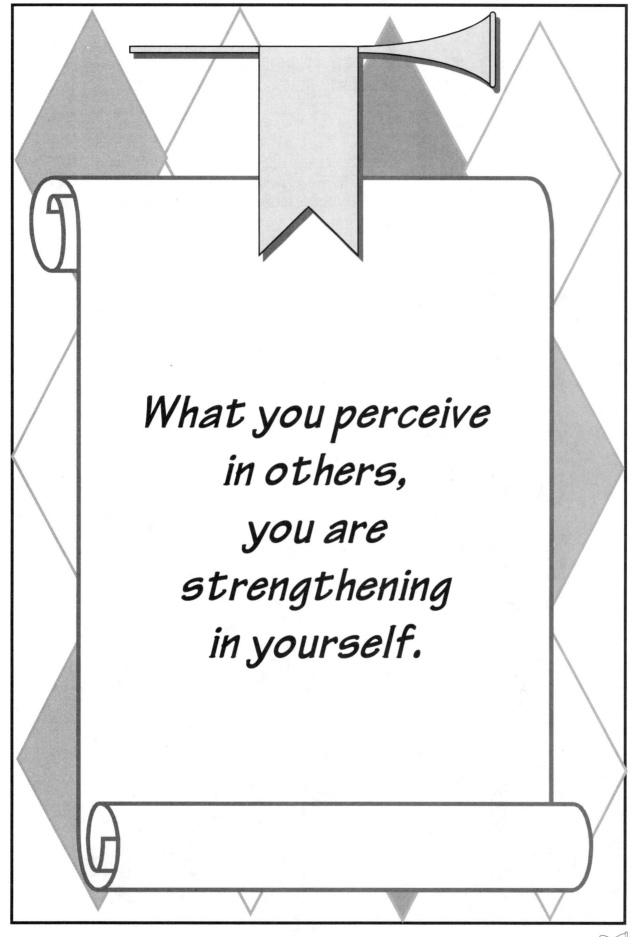

*What you perceive
in others,
you are
strengthening
in yourself.*

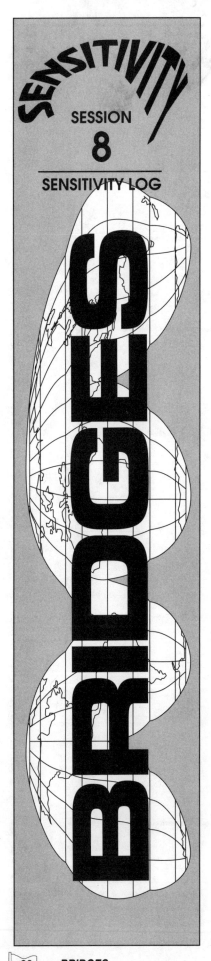

 ave students share what they have written on the Developing Sensitivity page of this book. Encourage positive comments from other members of the class.

At the end of this session, explain the following pages to the class. Tell the students that this is an on-going log of their actions showing sensitivity and the reactions of others. Set aside about 5 minutes each day, perhaps after lunch or recess, for students to record on these pages. Remind students to practice being sensitive to others and to be ready to record during the time period set aside.

Keep a log of the things you have done to show sensitivity to others.

DATE   TO WHOM   WHAT I DID

1. _____ _____ _____

                                    _____

2. _____ _____ _____

                                    _____

3. _____ _____ _____

                                    _____

4. _____ _____ _____

                                    _____

5. _____ _____ _____

                                    _____

6. _____ _____ _____

                                    _____

7. _____ _____ _____

                                    _____

List significant people in your life and how you are sensitive to them.

PERSON

HOW I AM SENSITIVE TO THIS PERSON

1. _____   _____
    _____

2. _____   _____
    _____

3. _____   _____
    _____

4. _____   _____
    _____

5. _____   _____
    _____

6. _____   _____
    _____

7. _____   _____
    _____

Here's your chance to keep a record of all the nice things people do for you!
Include classmates, teachers, brothers and sisters, parents, other adults, etc.

PERSON

WHAT THEY HAVE DONE FOR ME

1. _____

_____

_____

2. _____

_____

_____

3. _____

_____

_____

4. _____

_____

_____

5. _____

_____

_____

6. _____

_____

_____

7. _____

_____

_____

*Think of yourself
as you wish
others to
think of you.*

JDagobert D. Runes

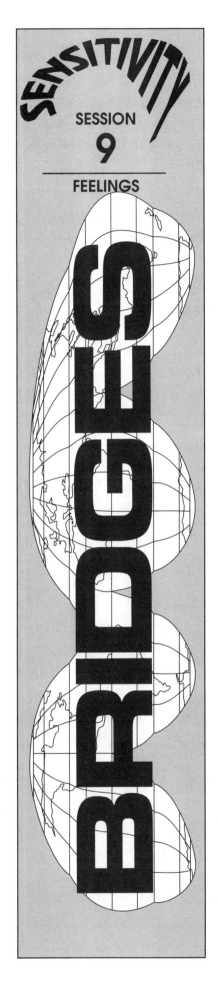

SENSITIVITY

SESSION
9

FEELINGS

BRIDGES

 ession 9 is designed to help students become aware of the multitude of feelings they may have and how those feelings are communicated to others.

PROCEDURE:

Read through each variation listed below. Before beginning any of the variations, have the class brainstorm a long list of emotions. Keep this list somewhere where everyone can see it, such as on the chalkboard, on an overhead transparency or on a chart.

Note: This session also could be used during the upcoming Communication sessions.

Variation #1:

Write each of the emotions previously brainstormed on separate pieces of paper. Turn the papers face down. Ask for a volunteer to choose one of the papers and act out the emotion written on it. He/She may use gestures, body language, facial expression, and/or special ways of moving to convey the feeling. The classmates then try to guess what emotion is being conveyed. Subsequent students can then volunteer, or the person who guessed an emotion gets to act out the next one.

Follow with a discussion of how people can communicate their feelings to each other without speaking. Ask students to see if they can come up with examples of real-life situations to which they should be sensitive.

Variation #2:

Alexander and the Terrible, Horrible, No-Good, Very Bad Day by Judith Viorst is a book that can be enjoyed at any age. Read this book aloud and then give students an opportunity to tell about their own terrible, horrible, no-good, very bad day in a creative writing assignment. When they've finished writing their stories, ask for volunteers to act out the emotions while the author reads his own story. After each skit, discuss how the terrible mishaps in their stories could have been prevented or handled in a better way.

BRIDGES 41

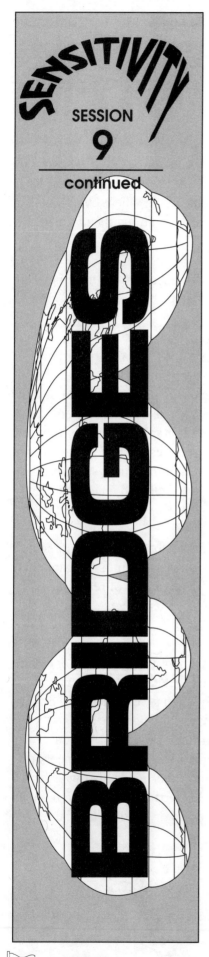

Variation #3:

Do a "round robin" story to illustrate the various emotions that a person might experience in a day. With the students sitting in a circle, begin telling a story about a very ordinary person who feels _____ when he/she wakes up because _____. For example, "One morning Bob's alarm rang. Lazily he reached over to turn it off so that he could go back to sleep. Suddenly he realized that today was the big day—the day he was going to show everyone how good he was in track! Today was Field Day! <u>Happily</u> he jumped out of bed and ran downstairs . . ." After one emotion has been mentioned, the story is passed on to the next student, either the next person in the circle or a volunteer. Give students the choice to continue the story or skip their turn if they wish.

Students continue the next portion of the story until another emotion has been mentioned, along with the reason for the emotion. This continues until the story comes to an end.

Follow with a discussion of how a person's feelings may change over the course of a day and how their feelings might affect other people. Students may enjoy talking about the story they just told—how their character handled various situations and how the character's mood might have been different if his/her attitude were different.

Variation #4:

Give students drawing paper and ask them to write the name of the emotion which could complete the following sentences.

> My dog is sick, and I feel ____. (sad)
> I got good grades, and I feel ____. (happy)
> I spilled my milk, and I feel ____. (sorry)
> I had a bad dream, and I feel ____. (scared)
> My sister pushed me, and I feel ____. (angry)
> I answered the question wrong. I feel ____. (stupid)
> I have a zit on my face. I feel ____. (embarrassed)

Now ask the students to make up their own sentences similar to the examples above which illustrate the meaning of different emotions.

Do not remove
a fly from
a friend's forehead
with a hatchet.

Chinese Proverb

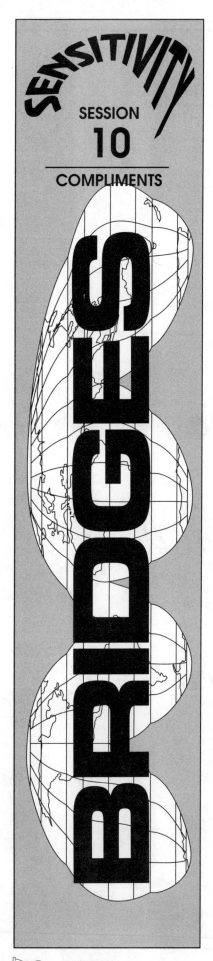

Everyone loves to hear good things about himself/herself. This activity will give everyone the opportunity to do so and to practice being sensitive to others as well. It also will provide a record of those good things for each student to keep.

MY COMPLIMENTS TO YOU

By now students should have developed an awareness of the good qualities of their classmates and a sensitivity to the good things they do. This exercise will give them an opportunity to share these realizations in a concrete manner.

Begin a discussion about how students feel when they are given a compliment. Talk about how a compliment means much more when it is specific, such as: "I really think it's neat the way you help other people in math without making them feel put down," rather than a vague "You're nice." Either, of course, is pleasant to hear, but the former is much more telling.

Touch on the difference between flattery, which is insincere, and compliments, which are heartfelt and show thought.

Begin the next activity by giving students a copy of the following page. They should write their name on the top line, then circulate it around the room to give and receive compliments. Give a certain period of time in which students are to complete the activity. (25-30 minutes may be a good period of time, or you may want to break it into two 15-minute sections.)

The rules for the activity are as follows:

- Sensitivity must be used. It is the keynote.
- Students may write on anyone else's paper.
- Students must write for anyone who asks them to do so.
- Students should value everyone's comments.

What's Great About . . .

_____

_____

_____

_____

_____

_____

_____

_____

_____

_____

_____

SENSITIVITY

Security is . . .
finding stability
in change.

JVM

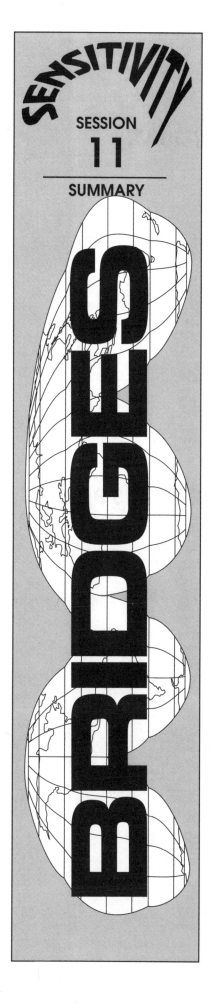

SENSITIVITY

BRIDGES

his is the final session on sensitivity, but it should be a subject you continue talking about throughout the year.

The following page is for students to summarize what they have learned about sensitivity and to make a plan to continue to grow in this area. They will be able to look at this page later in the year and evaluate the results of their performance of the plan.

Lead a class discussion about the sensitivity exercises and together look for examples of ways students can feel better about themselves and others. They can use the following page or their own sheet to keep and update as the years go by.

What I have learned about sensitivity

_____

_____

_____

_____

_____

What I must do to continue to grow in this area

_____

_____

_____

_____

_____

Any thoughts?
Put them here!

_____

_____

_____

_____

_____

_____

_____

_____

_____

_____

_____

_____

_____

_____

_____

_____

_____

_____

Things may come
to those who wait,
but only the things
left by those
who hustle.

Abraham Lincoln

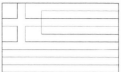

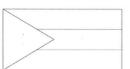

P A R T · T H R E E

Self-Esteem

Helping students better understand the concept of self-esteem

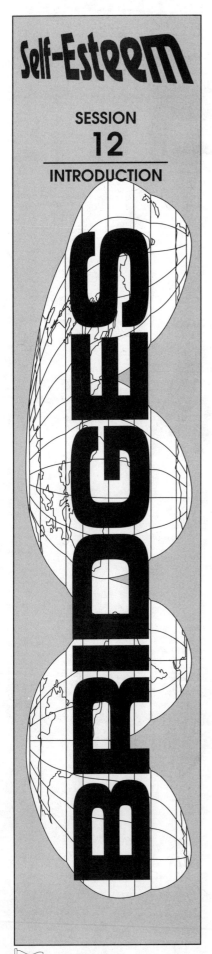

Self-Esteem

SESSION
12

INTRODUCTION

BRIDGES

ead page 53 with the group. Emphasize your own belief in the worth of every individual in the class. You may even want to point out some things that are special about certain people, especially those who tend to fade in a group. Let them know you care!

It's likely that many students will not be familiar with the word *self-esteem*, but they can understand that it means "how you feel about yourself." They can probably relate instances in their own lives when they were feeling really good as well as when they were feeling very down. One's self-esteem is how he views himself, which greatly affects how he reacts to the world.

Go over the questions on page 54. Students may fill in the blanks as the discussion is progressing or they may wait until after the discussion is finished.

End the lesson by re-emphasizing that everyone in the class is a worthwhile individual and that the goal of this chapter is attaining high self-esteem for all! Tell the students that it's an objective that can be accomplished best by working together.

1. Do you feel really good about yourself? _____

2. Are you usually glad that you are you instead of being someone else? _____

3. Could you make a list of all your strengths? _____

4. Are you proud of what you can accomplish? _____

If you answered "yes!" to these questions you have high self-esteem. That's great! You already know that you can contribute much to the group discussion.

If you answered "no" to any of these questions, then your self-esteem might be low. Now, that doesn't mean that you're not worthwhile. Quite the contrary! All it means is that you don't yet KNOW how special you are. As the class discusses self-esteem, you will become more aware of your importance as an individual.

High self-esteem for everyone

. . . that's the goal of this chapter. The best part is that we can all help each other attain it!

1. What is self-esteem?

_____

_____

_____

_____

2. How is self-esteem developed?

_____

_____

_____

3. How do you feel and act when you have high self-esteem?

_____

_____

_____

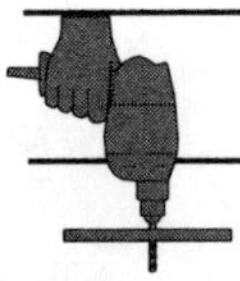

Self-Esteem

4. How do you feel and act when you have low self-esteem?

_____

_____

_____

5. How can you help someone else have better self-esteem?

_____

_____

6. How is someone's self-esteem hurt by others?

_____

_____

_____

1. What is self-esteem?

Self-esteem is the way you view yourself. High self-esteem shows in the way you feel about yourself in terms of having self-confidence, pride and a feeling of being worthy. Low self-esteem is just the opposite.

2. How is self-esteem developed?

Our sense of self-esteem comes from how we see ourselves and our abilities, through hearing what others say about us and how they act toward us, what we feel we are able to accomplish and contribute, etc.

3. How do you feel and act when you have high self-esteem?

You feel good about who and what you are. You are positive in your thinking and actions. You are happy and willing to take risks.

4. How do you feel and act when you have low self-esteem?

You are negative in your thoughts and actions. You feel down in the dumps and unable to accomplish much of what you really want to do. You feel that you are unworthy.

5. How can you help someone else have better self-esteem?

By showing that the person is worthy, by helping them develop a positive self-image, by helping them build on weaknesses to turn them into strengths, by saying meaningful, positive statements and by your positive actions toward that person.

6. How is someone's self-esteem hurt by others?

By people being negative toward someone, putting them down, giving backhanded or plastic compliments, ignoring them, treating them as unworthy of notice, being insensitive to their feelings, etc.

Whatever
is worth doing
at all,
is worth doing
well.

Lord Chesterfield

Those who
feel certain they
will not succeed
are seldom
mistaken.

Frances Osgood

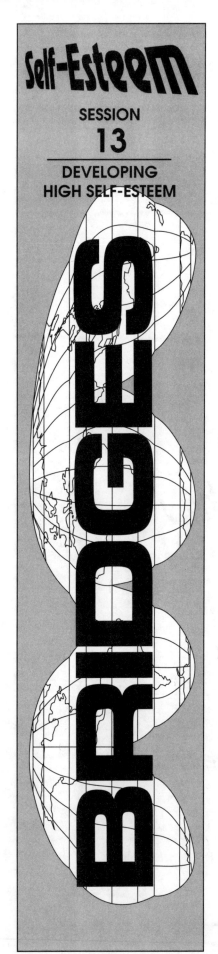

Self-Esteem

SESSION 13

DEVELOPING HIGH SELF-ESTEEM

his session is designed to help students see that what they think can make a major difference in what they can accomplish.

Read page 59 with the class. Emphasize the motto at the bottom of the page: think good thoughts! If students can get in the habit of stopping their negative thinking before they convince themselves that it's true, it will help them substantially.

After this page is discussed, follow through in class whenever you hear a student with a negative attitude about his/her abilities.

Assign page 62 to be completed by the next **Bridges** session.

End the class with a discussion on the saying . . .

If you think you can, or if you think you can't ... you're right!

HOW TO DEVELOP A HIGH Self-Esteem

Everyone has the right to feel good about himself. A person with high self-esteem knows exactly what his strengths are and acknowledges them with pride. He knows that hard work has given him strengths and that recognition is deserved for that. He's aware that he's been blessed with other abilities and doesn't unfairly judge others who may not have those abilities.

High self-esteem should not be confused with conceit. When a person is conceited, their opinion of themself is too high, and they feel overly important. They place themselves above others and brag about their personal strengths.

How does a person who has low self-esteem go about raising it? Well, the best way is to change his thought patterns. It's true — we feel the way we THINK we feel! If we're always thinking about how we can't do anything right, then that's usually what happens. However, if we decide to throw the word "can't" out of our everyday vocabulary, then we'll get a lot more done. If we don't know how to do something we can certainly learn! We need to remember that we just don't know how to do it YET!

THINK POSITIVE!

That's an important motto. If you find yourself thinking negative thoughts, mentally yell "STOP!" and then give yourself a pep talk. If you do this consistently, you will soon find that you are being more positive in everything you do. The more positive you are, the better you'll feel. And the better you feel, the higher your self-esteem will be.

GO FOR IT!

If you don't have confidence, you'll always find a way not to win.

Carl Lewis

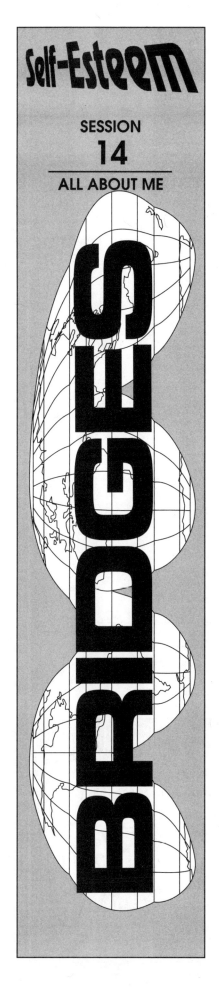

Self-Esteem

SESSION 14

ALL ABOUT ME

his session should be a fun time for the students to get to know one another a little better. They should be made to feel comfortable talking about what they have written on page 62.

You may want to make a game out of having them guess who else in the class might have the same response they do to specific questions.

Do not ask anything about a best friend as this may be a sensitive area for some of the children. It's possible that someone does not have many friends or that a person might think they're someone's best friend, and they're not.

Do not ask about being special during this session. That is taken up in detail in the next session.

ALL ABOUT **ME** AS OF THIS DATE

My name is_____

How I got my name _____

My address _____ Apt/Condo #_____

City _____

I live with _____

I'm _____ feet _____ inches tall.   I weigh _____ pounds.

The color of my hair is _____

The color of my eyes is _____

My favorite story/book is _____

My favorite color is_____

My favorite snack is_____

My favorite breakfast is_____

My favorite lunch is _____

My favorite dinner is _____

My favorite candy is _____and it costs_____

My favorite soda/pop is_____

The kind of music I like best is _____

My favorite music group is _____

My favorite song is_____

My favorite subject in school is_____

My favorite TV show is_____

In my free time, I like to_____

I do these extra activities outside of school_____

I like to play these sports_____

My favorite board game is_____

I have a pet _____ named_____

I like to collect_____

I'm special because_____

_____

Write additional facts about yourself on the back of this sheet.
(For example, if you have more than one pet, write that
information.)

Don't let life discourage you; everyone who got where he/she is had to begin where he/she was.

Richard Evans

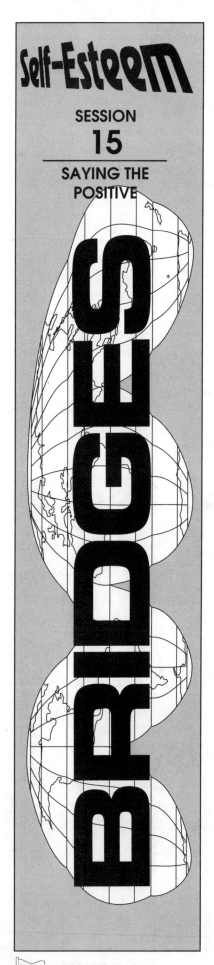

Self-Esteem

SESSION
15

SAYING THE POSITIVE

his session gives a chance for each individual to think about ways in which people can be special. The students should have already completed the previous <u>All About Me</u> page. However, it may have been difficult for some students because they do not view themselves in a positive light.

I'M SPECIAL

In this activity, students are going to be asked what they see as special about each other. They should volunteer their comments and direct them to the person involved. They will start the sentence with "You are special . . ." and then fill in a reason. Some examples are

. . . because of your red hair.
. . . because you are so neat in appearance.
. . . because you are well organized.
. . . because you have a horse.
. . . because you are kind/considerate/friendly/caring/polite.
. . . because you are always on time.
. . . because your work is always neat.
. . . because you play the piano/flute/drum.

Some students may wish to make their comment about someone who is not in the class, and that is fine. There are, however, obvious advantages to talking about class members who will hear the comment(s).

Note: *Be sure that students understand that all comments are to be positive. Emphasize how important it is for everyone to hear something good about himself. It is one way in which human beings develop high self-esteem.*

Follow this activity with a brief discussion of how students felt when others were saying positive things about them. Were they things that they expected or were they surprised by what others said?

*Make
good habits
and
they will
make you.*

Parks Cousins

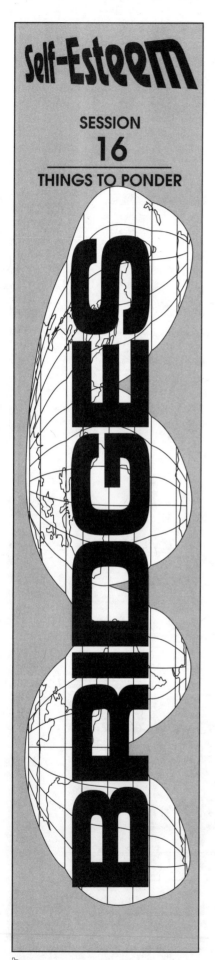

Through previous discussions involving both sensitivity and self-esteem, by now students should be aware that their actions and words influence other people. The following student page is designed to make them put these new thoughts into written words. You may want to go over the questions first so that you are sure students understand the meaning of each. You may ask them to give examples to illustrate what the questions are saying.

THINGS TO PONDER

1. How do positive thinking and acting affect my own self-esteem?

_____

_____

_____

2. How do I influence people?

_____

_____

_____

3. How do I make people feel?

_____

_____

_____

4. How do people react to my positive actions?

_____

_____

_____

5. How do people react to my negative actions?

_____

_____

_____

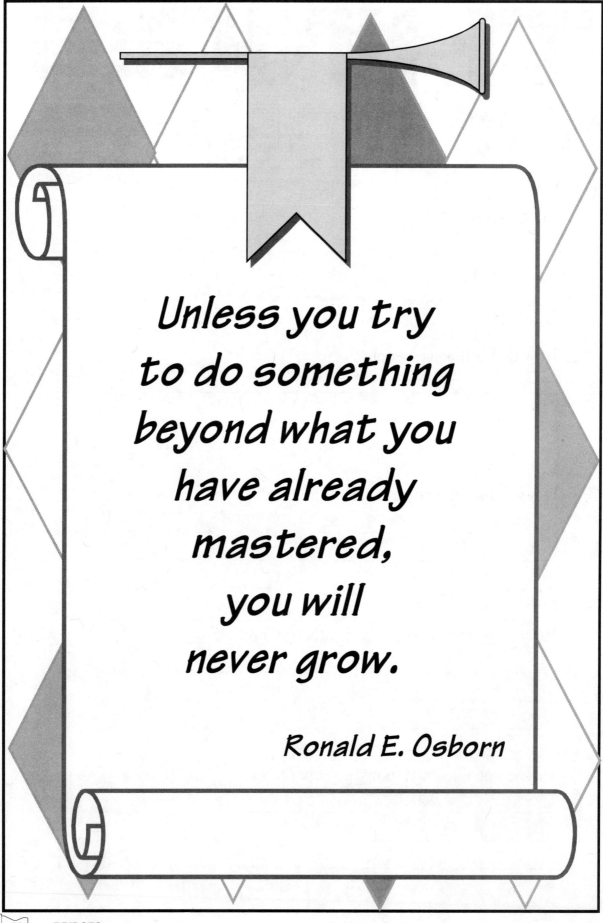

Unless you try to do something beyond what you have already mastered, you will never grow.

Ronald E. Osborn

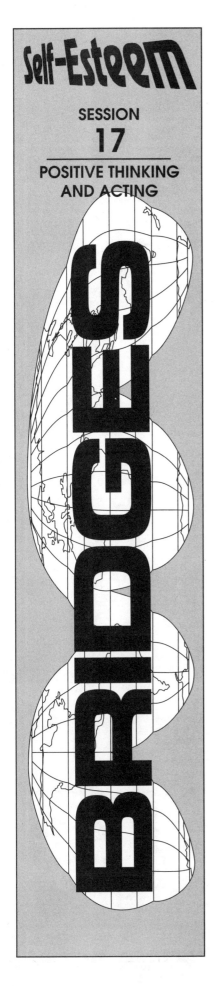

Self-Esteem

SESSION 17

POSITIVE THINKING AND ACTING

Tell students that page 70 is a brainstorm activity. Give them about 15 minutes in class to start their list of positive things they've done. They should write down as many things as they can possibly think of and then write some more! They may use the back of the paper as well.

Emphasize that in this activity they are asked to say what they do WELL. This is not bragging because they will not be writing things to impress other people. What they are doing is recognizing their strengths and things that make them unique. This is called self-assessment. It is not an act of conceit when students accurately list what they are good at doing.

When students are finished, they may read aloud some of their list. They may want to circle or check those of which they are most proud.

Positive + Thinking & Acting

List the positive things you have done.

1._____

2._____

3._____

4._____

5._____

6._____

These are your accomplishments!

If you can think of more . . . put them on the back!

Keep away from people who try to belittle your ambition. Small people always do that, but the really great make you feel that you, too, can become great.

Mark Twain

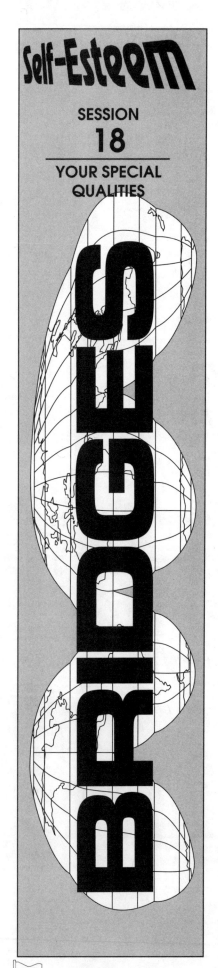

ight now you'll have a chance to play this variation of an old game. It requires players to remember what each "packed" for a trip. In this version students will remember positive qualities about each other.

With students sitting in a circle, the first one says, "My name is _____ and I am special because . . ." where she adds a positive statement about herself. The next person in the circle starts the same way, but after a statement about himself, he must repeat the statement each previous person made. This continues around the circle.

If someone "misses," or cannot remember everyone's statement, it is advised that the game not be stopped. Instead, elicit help from other members of the group. It is important that each person gets to hear his/her own special quality being said by the others.

An example of the game would go like this:
- #1: My name is Jennifer and I am special because I always try to be kind.
- #2: My name is Dan and I am special because I am very good at sports, and Jennifer always tries to be kind.
- #3: My name is Fred and I am special because I am a good worker, and Dan is very good at sports, and Jennifer always tries to be kind.
- #4: My name is Sue and I am special because I am good at writing, and Fred is a good worker, and Dan is very good at sports, and Jennifer always tries to be kind.

Each player should be pointed to as their name is mentioned.

Note: *One service the teacher can consider is to seat those with the lowest self-esteem and/or poorest memory at the beginning of the circle.*

It still may be difficult for some members to come up with a special quality about himself/herself. In this case the teacher and the other players can find positive things to say about that person. It's important, however, that the flow of the game is not interrupted by frequent situations such as this. Perhaps the teacher could verify that each student has thought of something to say before the game begins.

I've decided to stick with love. Hate is too great a burden to bear.

Martin Luther King, Jr.

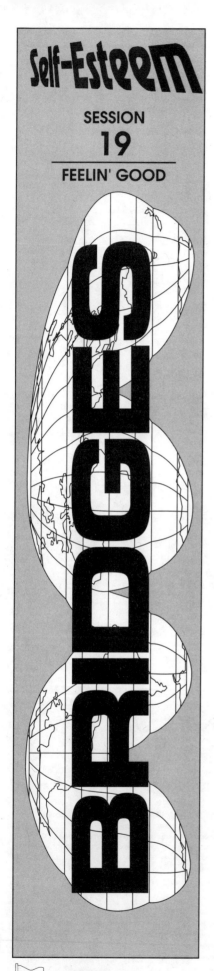

Self-Esteem

SESSION
19

FEELIN' GOOD

BRIDGES

his session simply introduces the log pages which follow. Look at them with the class and discuss the types of entries students might make. Give them several minutes to write.

After students have written on the first two pages, ask them to turn to the "I Put a Smile on Someone's Face" page. On this page students will write on someone else's page rather than their own. They will write what that person has done to make them smile. Students should not ask to write on someone else's page but rather must be asked to write on it. It will take the initiative of the receiver to have their kindnesses and good deeds recognized. It will become a special record for that student to keep.

At the end of the session remind students that these log pages are ongoing and that they should continue to write on them whenever appropriate.

PEOPLE

WHO MADE
ME
FEEL GOOD ABOUT
MYSELF

Here's your chance to keep a record of the people who helped make your day/week/month a little better than it would have been otherwise.

Date   <u>Who</u> Made Me Feel Good and <u>How</u> They Did It

1. _____ _____

_____

2. _____ _____

_____

3. _____ _____

_____

4. _____ _____

_____

5. _____ _____

_____

6. _____ _____

_____

7. _____ _____

_____

PEOPLE

WHO
I
MADE FEEL GOOD
ABOUT THEMSELVES

Also, keep a record of the people who you helped make their day/week/month a little better than it would have been otherwise.

Date	Who I Made Feel Good and How I Did It
1. _____	_____
	_____
2. _____	_____
	_____
3. _____	_____
	_____
4. _____	_____
	_____
5. _____	_____
	_____
6. _____	_____
	_____
7. _____	_____
	_____

I PUT A Smile on someone's face!

_____

_____

_____

_____

_____

_____

_____

_____

_____

_____

_____

The secret
of happiness
is not in doing
what one likes,
but in liking
what one does.

James M. Barrie

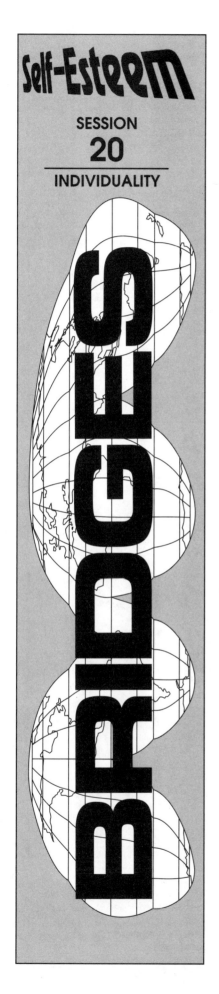

Self-Esteem

SESSION
20
INDIVIDUALITY

his session is a chance for each student to display something positive about himself/ herself to the rest of the class.

This activity should follow a discussion of the reasons we appreciate individuality. Students should understand that it is important and beneficial that we are not alike in the way we look, act, think and dress. Diversity means being different. We are all individuals and can grow as such and learn to respect and appreciate the uniqueness of all people.

In addition, students should talk about how advertising is used in our society to display the positive qualities of products to make them appealing to many people.

Note: *Perhaps these discussions could be tied together by talking about how freedom of choice is limited in other countries.*

LET ME TELL YOU ABOUT ME

Give students a 12" x 18" sheet of white construction paper on which they will make a poster advertising themselves by stressing their positive qualities. They may cut out old magazine pictures for a collage about their positive qualities, or they may draw with bright colors on the paper.

Finish the session with each student telling their classmates about their poster. Display the posters in the room afterwards.

Variation #1: A large sheet of paper which covers the bulletin board could be divided into puzzle-piece sections. (Be sure you number the pieces on the back and make a diagram so you'll be able to reassemble the puzzle later.) Each student can use one "puzzle piece" to advertise himself/herself, being sure to include his/her name on the poster. When everyone is finished, reassemble the puzzle. This is a good springboard for a discussion about how everyone is unique but each contributes to make the puzzle complete.

Variation #2: Instead of posters or puzzle pieces, individual flags or coats-of-arms could be designed.

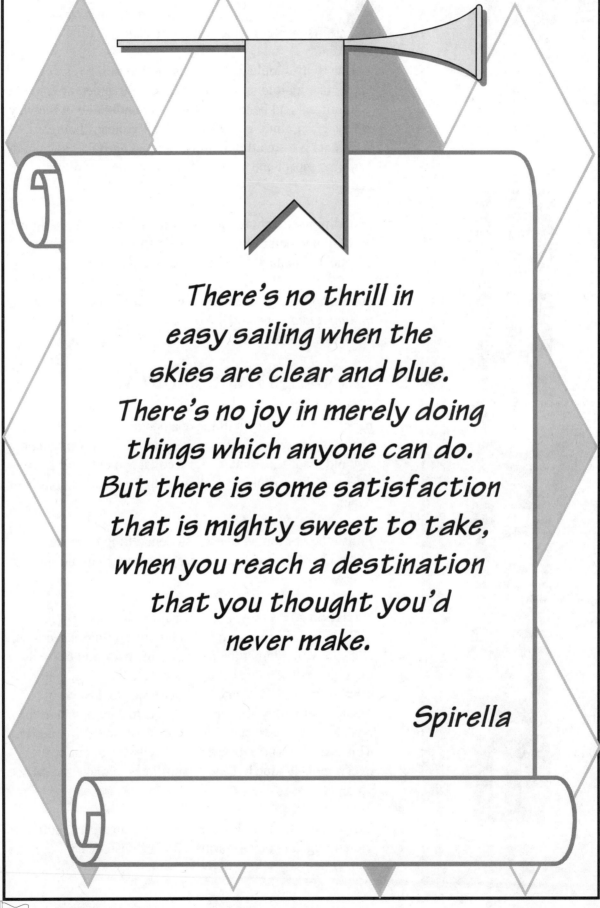

There's no thrill in
easy sailing when the
skies are clear and blue.
There's no joy in merely doing
things which anyone can do.
But there is some satisfaction
that is mighty sweet to take,
when you reach a destination
that you thought you'd
never make.

Spirella

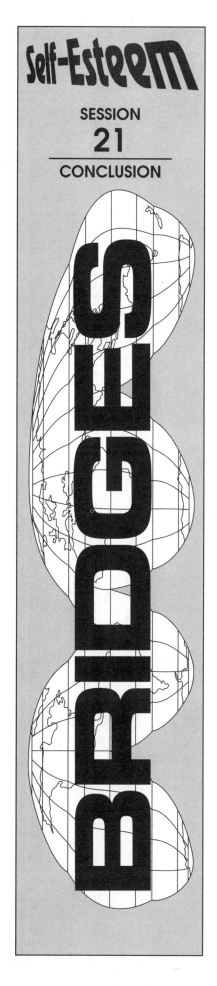

Self-Esteem

SESSION
21
CONCLUSION

BRIDGES

or the final session on self-esteem, ask students to react to what they have learned. Specifically, ask them to tell the ways in which they feel they have raised their self-esteem and/or helped others to do so.

This is also a good time to have a discussion about the relationship between sensitivity and self-esteem.

Following the class discussion, allow students time to complete the following student page. For the second and third questions, stress that they should be making a plan instead of writing vague remarks. Give examples such as "I will yell 'STOP' to myself when I'm thinking negatively," and "I will make a point to tell others what I like about them."

Plan to return to the following page at the end of the year so that students can see how well they're adhering to their plan.

Review:

What have I learned about self-esteem?

_____

_____

_____

_____

The Plan:

What do I need to do to continue to have a positive self-esteem?

_____

_____

_____

_____

How can I help others continue to grow in their positive self-esteem?

_____

_____

_____

**Any thoughts?
Put them here!**

There is no way to happiness. Happiness is the way.

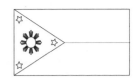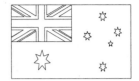

P A R T • F O U R

Communication

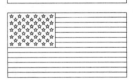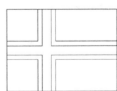

Helping students learn the art

of effective communication

with teachers, parents and

fellow students

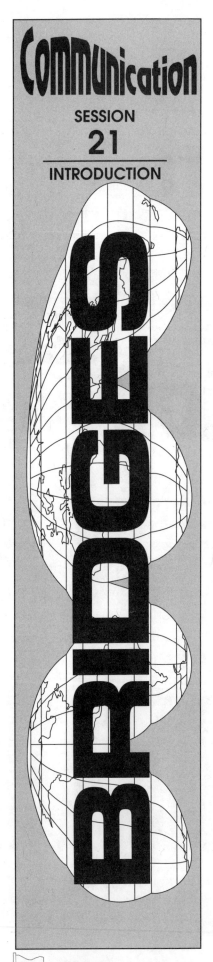

 egin this session by reading page 87. You may want to give students some simple instructions in sign language or some other "irregular" form of communication. That will give you a good start on the chapter.

When you've discussed the first student page, go over the questions on the page following it. The students may write their answers as you discuss the questions, or you may choose to have them do it following the discussion.

When you've finished these assignments, be sure to direct the group's attention to the TO DO note at the bottom of the page. Give them a due date of the next **Bridges** sesson so they will bring their bags to class on that day. Remind them not tell anyone what's in their bag.

Communication

- Do you watch people's faces and body language when they talk for clues about what they're really saying?
- Have you ever noticed how many different ways people can communicate with each other?
- Have you ever tried to say something that just didn't come out right?
  - Have your ever felt that the way you asked for something had a lot to do with whether or not you got it?
    - Did you know that listening is a major part of communication? After all, how can you really communicate with another person if you haven't heard what he/she has said?

Our ability to communicate is one of our most important assets. Just think about it— we can talk about ideas and abstract things as well as things we can actually see and touch. Animals can communicate, but they can't do it nearly as well as people can. We are gifted with this awesome, unique ability!

You may have noticed that some people are better at communicating than others. If we can learn how to communicate effectively, we will find other people more anxious to hear what we have to say. In this chapter we're going to learn how to say exactly what we mean . . . and the most effective way of saying it!

So, hold on to your seats — you're going to have a lot of fun learning some new communication skills.

✉ What is communication? _____

_____

_____

☎ Why is it important that the message is understood? _____

_____

_____

📖 Name some means or methods of communicating. _____

_____

_____

💻 Give some examples of the following types of communication:

Verbal _____

Nonverbal _____

Symbolic _____

🏳 How do we communicate about ourselves? _____

_____

_____

To the next **Bridges** session bring in a paper sack with something (anything) in it from home. Don't tell anyone what is in it! We'll be using the secret items for a communication game.

Communication

✉ What is communication?_____

Communication is any method by which we give information to each other, exchange thoughts, make something known. Good communication involves listening, hearing, paying attention, understanding and responding appropriately.

☎ Why is it important that the message is understood?_____

If we understand the words, but do not respond to the "message" we have not actually communicated. Communication is a two-way street.

📖 Name some means or methods of communicating._____

By conversation, letter writing, books, television, FAX, computers, signal flags, Morse Code, sign language, traffic lights, signs, etc.

💻 Give some examples of the following types of communication:

Verbal ___Talking, singing, writing, acting, story telling, etc._____

Nonverbal ___Facial expressions, body language, gestures, dance, pictures, etc.___

Symbolic ___Sign language, traffic signs, art, internationally recognized symbols (like a circle with a diagonal line that means "not allowed"), etc.___

🏳 How do we communicate about ourselves?_____

_____

_____

To the next **Bridges** session bring in a paper sack with something (anything) in it from home. Don't tell anyone what is in it! We'll be using the secret items for a communication game.

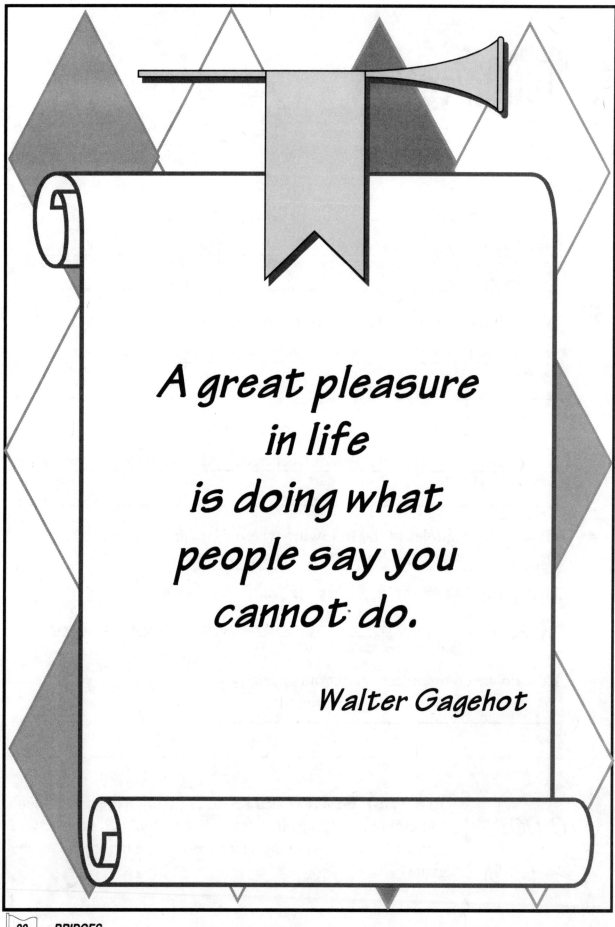

A great pleasure
in life
is doing what
people say you
cannot do.

Walter Gagehot

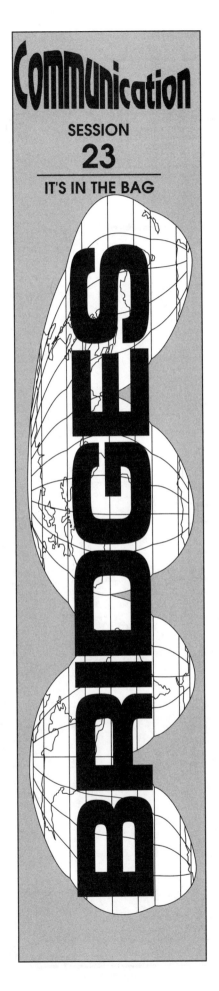

Communication

Students were asked during the last **Bridges** session to bring an item from home in a paper sack. Each student should be given an opportunity to communicate to the rest of the class what he's brought in, without directly telling them what it is.

There are two ways to do this exercise. The student may begin to describe it and let the group guess until they guess correctly what it is, or the class may play "20 Questions," asking yes and no questions to discover the object's identity.

*People are
lonely because
they build walls
instead of
bridges.*

J.F. Newton

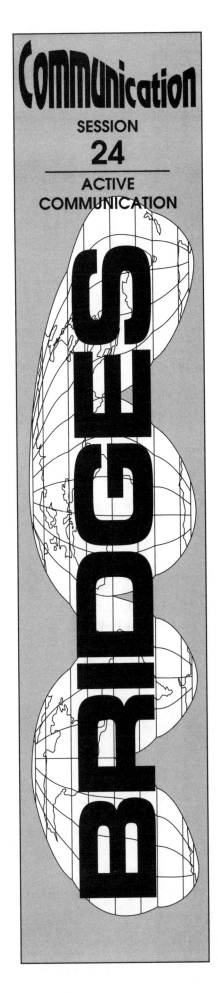

Communication

SESSION
24

ACTIVE COMMUNICATION

BRIDGES

ead the next page as a class. The page is an outline for a simple, easy-to-follow plan for dealing with a common situation: asking permission to go somewhere.

When you have finished reading and discussing the exercise, do some role playing of different situations, i.e. going to a movie, to the mall, to a friend's house, to a sleepover, asking for a ride to get school supplies or asking for help with a math problem.

You may want to demonstrate the "wrong" way of doing this. Give incomplete information on where you want to go, then demand rather than ask to go. Briefly discuss why it was an ineffective method of communication, then have the students compare your demonstration with a more correct way to communicate. For which request would they be most likely to grant permission? Can they see both a parent's viewpoint and a child's viewpoint?

Emphasize that their tone of voice and choice of words may make a big difference to the person from whom they are asking permission.

After doing a few role plays, ask the "adult" in the situation to deny permission and challenge the students to react in a befitting manner. Discuss the reasons why their reaction to a "no" answer should be respectful.

EFFECTIVE COMMUNICATION

 ffective, active communication includes listening to what the other person is saying as well as communicating exactly what you want to say.

Say exactly what you mean and say it nicely!

Think about asking permission to go somewhere. If you're including the following information, you will be effectively communicating what is needed in order for permission to be granted.

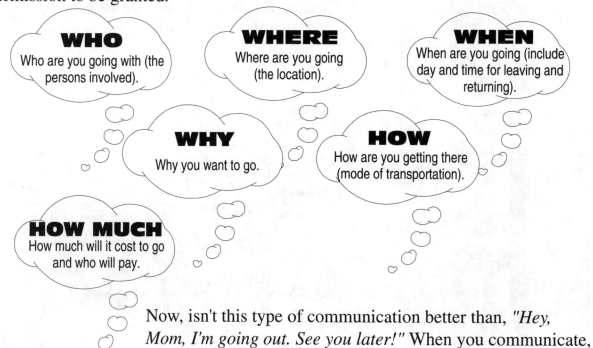

WHO
Who are you going with (the persons involved).

WHERE
Where are you going (the location).

WHEN
When are you going (include day and time for leaving and returning).

WHY
Why you want to go.

HOW
How are you getting there (mode of transportation).

HOW MUCH
How much will it cost to go and who will pay.

Now, isn't this type of communication better than, *"Hey, Mom, I'm going out. See you later!"* When you communicate, you should also be sensitive. That means that you are listening and reacting with respect to what the other person is saying.

Most of us have more courage than we ever dreamed we possessed.

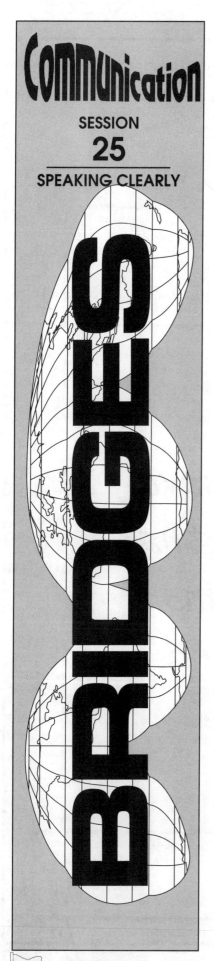

Communication

SESSION 25

SPEAKING CLEARLY

BRIDGES

W e have all had experiences where we simply did not hear correctly what another person was saying. It may be that he did not speak clearly ... or maybe we were only half listening! This activity will help students see what can happen when there is poor communication.

Open a discussion with students about times that they did not communicate effectively with someone and what consequences resulted. If possible, get a tape of Abbott and Costello's famous "Who's on First?" routine to play for the class to hear.

As a class, brainstorm a telephone conversation between a mother and child. The conversation should be full of miscommunications.

Example:

Child says:	Mother hears:
I just broke an egg.	I just broke my leg.
Then I had a call.	Then I had a fall.
I got lunch from a friend.	I got punched by a friend.
I burned a pan.	I burned my hand.

After you have talked about how these miscommunications happened and the resulting panicked mother, divide the students into small groups. Give them an opportunity to write brief plays in which miscommunication is the key theme.

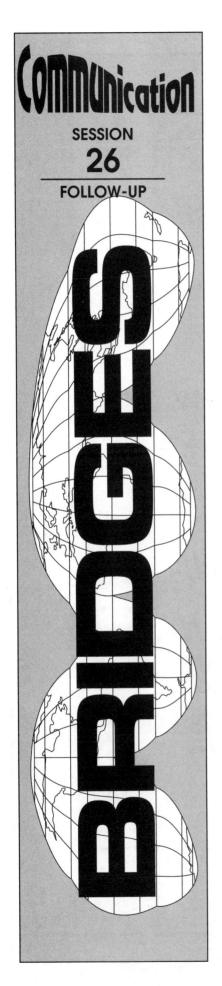
 ave the students share their plays with the others. This can be done by either reading or actually acting out the parts.

Follow-up should include a discussion about how this may be funny to watch in a play but how the possible consequences in real life could be disastrous. Review some of the plays and talk about the parts where one or more of the characters could have prevented the miscommunication. Discuss pertinent questions that the characters could have asked each other to help clarify the situations.

Do not follow where the path may lead. Go instead where there is no path and leave a trail.

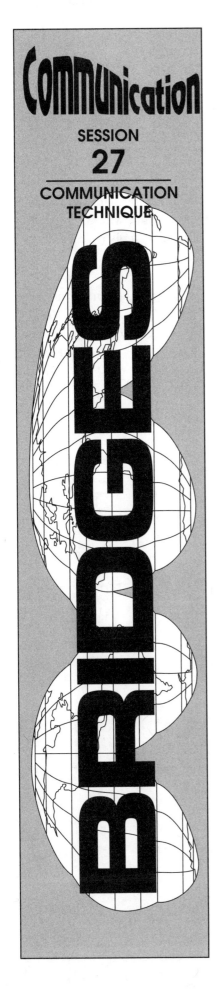

Communication

BRIDGES

 tart this session by reminding students of the plays they just wrote and the disasterous results of miscommunication. Tell them that today they are going to learn how to avoid making those mistakes.

The class should turn to the next page and read aloud the procedure, discussing it as they go.

Then go back over the main points, which are:

1. REPEATING what a person says verifies his/her meaning.

2. REPHRASING is a technique that lets the person know that you are listening to her. It involves putting what she is saying into your own words and still letting her continue with the conversation.

Be sure that the class knows that repeating and rephrasing are not done constantly because that would be annoying. We *repeat* what the person says when there are important details involved that we need to make sure we know. We *rephrase* what the person says when we are listening in a sensitive, active manner and we want the person to feel our empathy for him/her. This can be any emotion, positive or negative. We share both sadness and joy with others.

When you have finished discussing the procedure, go on to Communication Guidelines. Stress to students that when someone is telling them about a problem, one of the most effective things they can do is just listen. That is often more helpful than constantly proposing solutions and certainly more helpful than belittling the importance of the problem.

You may want to do some informal role playing to illustrate the techniques. Here are some suggestions:

• Your friend is really feeling happy about his new bike and he's telling you about it. You sound like you feel great, saying you're glad to see he's so happy.

• Three of you are making plans to meet at the theater. Ask what movie you want to see, when is it playing and where. Do you have permission to go and how much will it cost? When all the information is determined, then it must be repeated so that each person knows exactly what is happening.

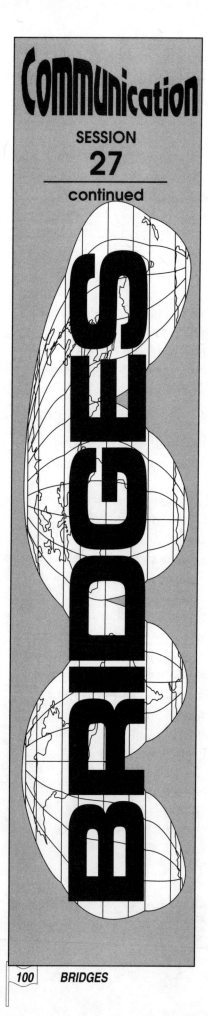

- There's a party that your friend wants to attend, but she also wants to go to her grandmother's that day. There's no way she can do both because her grandmother lives out of town. She's telling you about it. You can see that she is having a rough time making a decision and how hard it is for her.

- Your older sister can't find anyone to be with on Saturday. It's tough that no one is home, and you know she'll miss her friends. You know how that feels because it happens to you sometimes, too.

- Your mother is in charge of a big social event at the church, and she's afraid that it won't be a success. You notice how nervous she is, but you know she's done a good job organizing it. It was a big responsibility for her, and you know she probably won't relax until it's over.

A Communication Technique

Try this!
You'll find that more people are seeking you out because you are such a good conversationalist. That means you're actually a good listener!

*I*t's important that we know whether or not we are really understanding what someone is saying to us and vice versa. There's a really simple way to assure ourselves of this, and that is by repeating what the person said!

It's fairly easy to talk with someone when the subject does not involve anything personal or abstract. We need to keep the "facts" in mind and be certain that they're all understood. For example, if someone makes arrangements to meet you somewhere, repeat back to him/her the place, date, time and any other plans that were made for the meeting. That way you'll be certain that you've both understood the situation to be exactly the same. One of you won't arrive an hour before the other and at a different location!

You can also use the technique of repeating in conversations that involve someone's feelings. For example, if a friend tells you that he's sick and tired of his little brother bothering him all the time, you may say something like this: "Yea, I can tell he really bugs you." This kind of repeating, or rephrasing*, lets the person know that you are really listening to him. It also allows him to continue with what he is saying, knowing that someone is actually hearing what's being said. That feels good!

* Rephrasing is putting what the other person is saying into your own words. That allows both of you to recognize whether there has been understanding of what's been said.

COMMUNICATION
Guidelines

Here are some "rules" for communicating effectively that will help you.

1.
Listen to the thought as well as the words. Respond to the person's feelings.

2.
Be sensitive in what you say.
Speak to people the way you would like to be spoken to.

3.
Don't argue over little things or correct people on something that doesn't matter.

4.
When having a conversation, really listen to what the other person is saying.
Don't be planning what you're going to say next.

5.
Be honest, but don't constantly express your opinions
when no one has asked for them.

6.
Don't be judgmental or always try to outdo the other person.
Let people take pride in their accomplishments
without being put down.

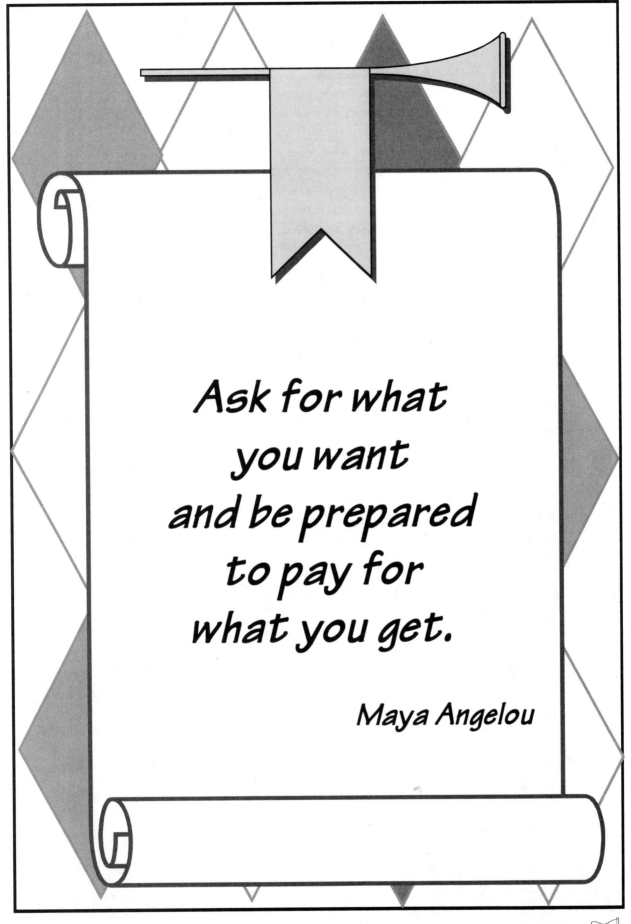

*Ask for what
you want
and be prepared
to pay for
what you get.*

Maya Angelou

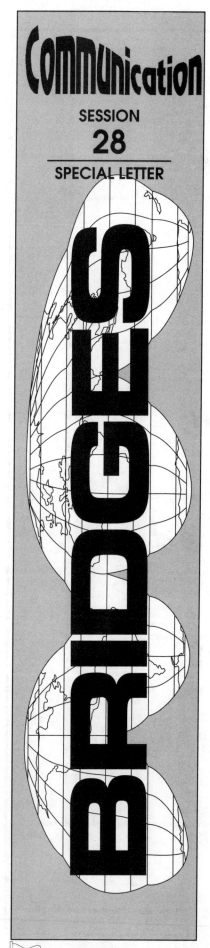

his next activity is very special and one in which students will find meaning. It's important that they are motivated to do a terrific job on it.

Read over page 105 with the students so that they are aware of what's going to happen to the letters. Emphasize that they will not be seeing their letter for a long period of time, so it's a chance for the NOW person they are to communicate with the FUTURE person they will become. If they sincerely concentrate on what they're writing, it will be a real thrill for them to get their letter later on. If they hurry through this, there is no doubt they will be very disappointed later. Give students plenty of time to get a good start on this letter in class. If they don't finish it, they may take it home to complete.

It is your option to retain these letters or give them to the students. There are advantages both ways. If you keep the letter, it will be more of a surprise for them to get it later and there's no chance they will have peeked at it. The disadvantages, of course, are that some students will have moved without giving you their forwarding address, and also you'll have to keep track of the letters for years!

Here are some suggestions if you decide to keep the letters yourself:

- Make certain that students bring in double the amount of postage that is currently required. Otherwise inflation could take its toll on your budget in several years when you go to mail the letters.

- Put all the letters in a large manila envelope plainly marked with the date they are to be mailed. Store it in a safe place where you won't forget it!

- When you mail the letters, enclose a letter of your own telling the students where you are and what you are currently doing. You'll be delighted at the number of them who write back to you to let you know how much getting the letter meant to them!

A Special Letter
TO YOURSELF!

This activity will be lots of fun for you to do, especially if you really put some thought into it.

You're going to write a letter to YOURSELF! Does that sound crazy? Maybe, but it's certain you will enjoy reading it years from now. The letter will be put away to be mailed back to you later.

The letter will contain some of the items below as they are right now. Many years from now you'll read the letter and see how things have changed or remained the same.

You may include

- **How you "see" yourself as a person, a student and a member of your family.**
- **What you like best about yourself.**
- **What you would like to change about yourself.**
- **Who your best friends are and why you like them.**
- **What your favorite TV shows, movies, music, sports, meals, etc. are.**
- **What you would do if you had all the money you could ever use/spend.**
- **What problems you have and how you think they'll be resolved.**
- **What you think you will be doing after you graduate from high school.**
- **What you think you will be doing in 10 years, 15 years.**
- **What you would like to do as a career.**
- **Anything else that you consider important about you.**

See the following page for what to do with the finished letter.

A Special Letter

CONTINUED

When you're finished with the letter, put it in an envelope and seal it. Address it to yourself on the outside and put the date it should be mailed (or read) in the lower left-hand corner. The date could be when you will graduate from high school or college or simply a number of years from now.

Give the letter to someone you know (perhaps your teacher) who can contact you at that later date. You could have a parent hold onto it in a safe place, too. If you give it to someone to mail to you, be sure to put two postage stamps on the envelope. If you move, remember to give your new address to that person.

Regardless of who keeps the envelope for you, you should not read your letter until the date you wrote on the outside. Just think how great it will be to receive a letter from yourself! You'll be able to reach back into your past and see how you felt in elementary school. It will also be interesting to find out how many of your predictions came true. You will be able to see the ways in which you stayed the same and the ways in which you changed.

In this letter, express your true feelings and thoughts. Remember, only <u>you</u> will be seeing this letter. Many years from now it will be great to have this letter to share with your own kids!

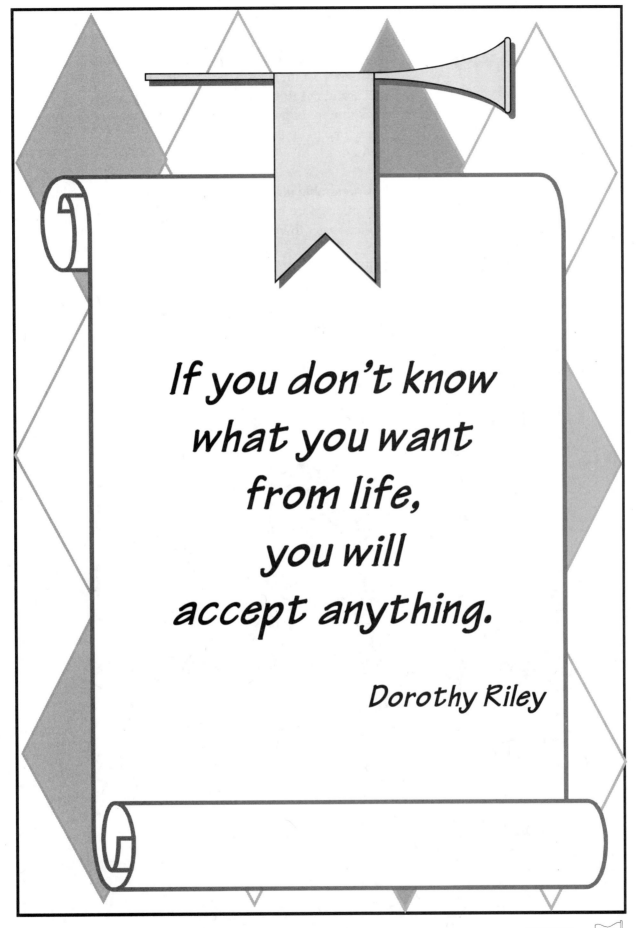

*If you don't know
what you want
from life,
you will
accept anything.*

Dorothy Riley

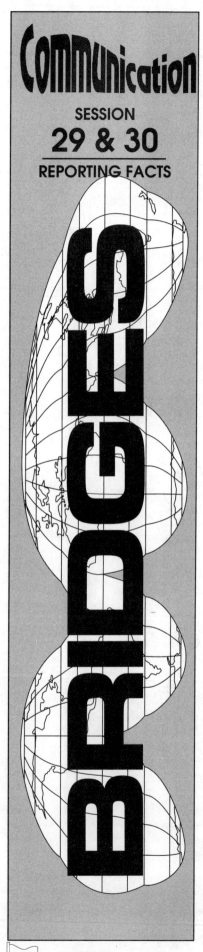

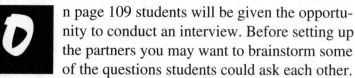

On page 109 students will be given the opportunity to conduct an interview. Before setting up the partners you may want to brainstorm some of the questions students could ask each other. Be careful not to do too many for a good part of this activity is thinking up the questions. Students should be given some time to do this on their own before they get with their partner.

It is preferable that students are not matched with someone they already are well acquainted with. This will give them a chance to get to know someone else in the class better.

This activity will take two sessions, one (Session 29) for making up the questions and conducting the interviews and the second (Session 30) for students to "introduce" their partner to the class. Each introduction should be relatively brief but contain as much information as possible. The accuracy of the information will convey how well the classmates communicated in their interviews.

REPORTING THE
FACTS

You are a reporter doing an interview with a classmate. Write down the questions you think are important to ask so that you'll be ready to introduce the classmate to other students. Leave enough space after each question to record the answer too!

_____

_____

_____

_____

_____

_____

_____

_____

_____

_____

At the next session, introduce your new friend to the rest of the class. Be sure that he/she tells you if you got all your facts correct.

Mind if I ask you just a few questions?

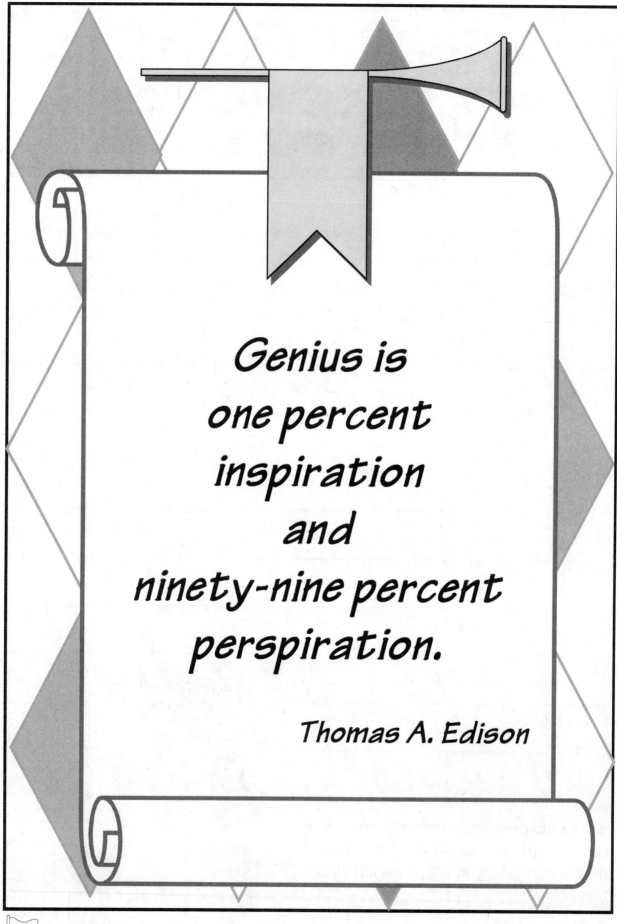

Genius is
one percent
inspiration
and
ninety-nine percent
perspiration.

Thomas A. Edison

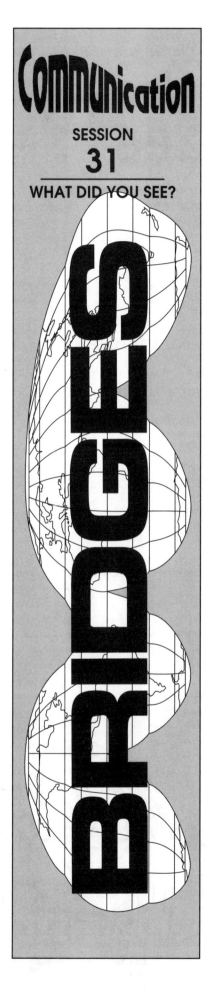

Communication

SESSION
31

WHAT DID YOU SEE?

he following activity requires advance preparation in secrecy. As the teacher, you should set up a situation to take place at a certain time and place so that all your students will observe it. Perhaps it will be an argument in which selected participants hurl all sorts of taunts and accusations at each other. It should be relatively brief, but plausible and somewhat chaotic and confusing. The actors should then exit the scene.

After the scene is over quickly pass out copies of page 112 and tell the students to write down everything they saw. If they need extra room they may continue on the back.

When everyone is finished bring the actors back into the room and go over exactly what happened. Have the class evaluate what they wrote by finishing page 108.

Follow up with a discussion of what students saw accurately and what they missed. Relate this to the importance of being specific when communicating.

What Did You See ?

_____

_____

_____

_____

_____

_____

_____

_____

_____

_____

_____

_____

_____

_____

_____

I was right about:

_____

_____

_____

_____

_____

I was not right about:

_____

_____

_____

_____

I think the reason I was not correct was

_____

_____

_____

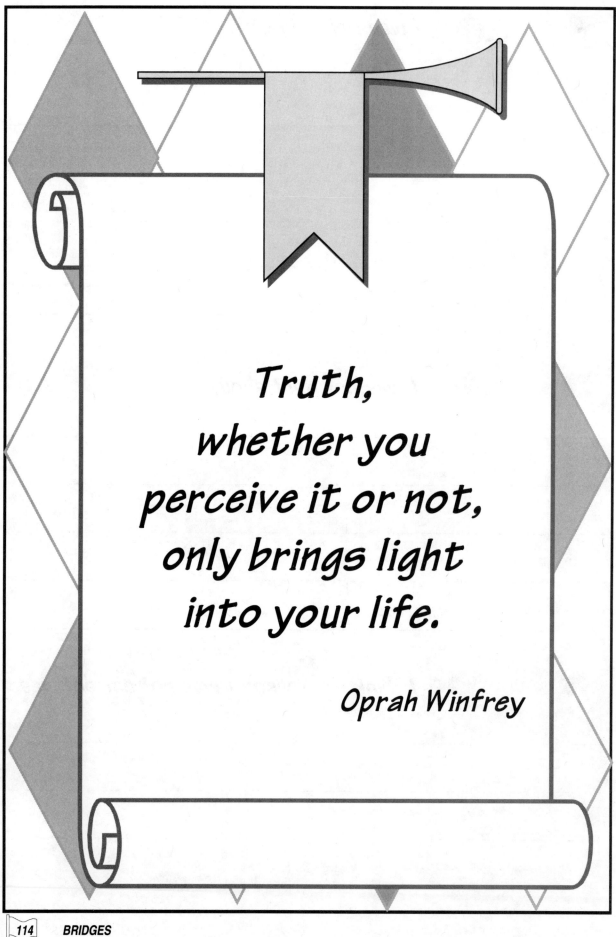

Truth,
whether you
perceive it or not,
only brings light
into your life.

Oprah Winfrey

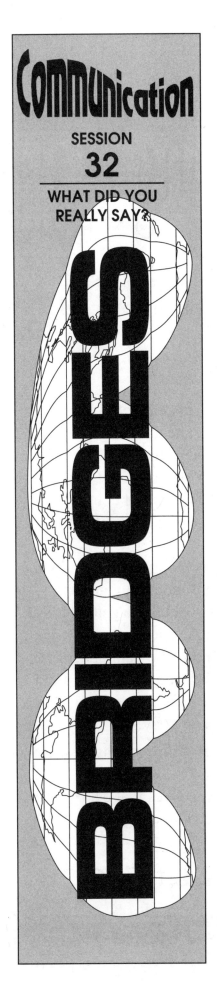

 his session deals with the fact that sometimes what people say is the exact opposite of what they are really feeling.

Pass out copies of pages 116 and 117, and read page 116 aloud with the class. Discuss the questions that are presented and ask students if they can recall examples of a time when they did what the paragraphs illustrate. Most of them will be able to do so.

Review the possible replies on page 117 and discuss each of them with the class. See if they can think of other scenarios and evaluate those too, based on sensitivity and respect.

What's Really Being Said?

Have you ever said something that was the exact opposite of what you really meant? Of course you have! Everyone has! It's not that you're lying, it's just that for some reason you weren't comfortable saying precisely what you were feeling.

Let's look at some examples:

- A friend's team has just lost an important football game that would have taken them to the championship tournament. Your friend says to you, "Oh, who cares about going to a lousy tournament anyway? It doesn't matter."

- A girl in your class always gets very high marks, but on one particular test she doesn't score as well as she had expected. Her reaction? "Oh, well, I'll still get an A for the quarter. You know, I didn't even study for this test, so it's no wonder I didn't get as high a grade as usual. I could have done better if I'd wanted to."

- A boy is being threatened by the neighborhood bully and the threats seem to be getting closer to being carried out. After one incident the boy announces to you, "I'm not afraid of that big guy. He's all hot air. I could beat him up any day!"

Do you think these people are saying what they really feel? Why or why not? If you think they are saying the opposite of what they really feel, why do you think they do this? For example are they trying to convince themselves that everything is OK, making others think that they're handling it better, or "whistling in the dark?" What other explanations do you have for this behavior?

What should you do in these situations?

Go on to the next page to find out.

What's Really Being Said?

Here are some possible replies:

➡ "Well, I know how you really feel, and you're lying now. You care a lot and you know it!"
(This reply is insensitive and doesn't allow the person his pride.)

➡ "Yea, I'll just bet that's what you think."
(This implies the person is lying and is also insensitive and unkind.)

➡ "Hey, I agree with you. It's no big deal."
(This is a better response because it offers support and allows the person to keep his/her pride. However, it does not lead to any further discussion that the person may want, even though he/she isn't saying so.)

➡ "If I were you, I'd be disappointed (or scared, etc.). However, you seem to be handling it well. What are your plans now?"
(This reply is best because it reaffirms what the person is saying, yet allows him/her to continue the discussion. By asking what his/her plans are now, you are taking positive steps.)

Discuss each of these replies. Can you think of other good responses?

> **In order to communicate
> we have to be good listeners
> as well as good speakers!
> We need to let others know
> that we care about what they are saying.**

*Some see things
as they are and say,
"Why?"
I dream things that
never were and say,
"Why not?"*

George Bernard Shaw

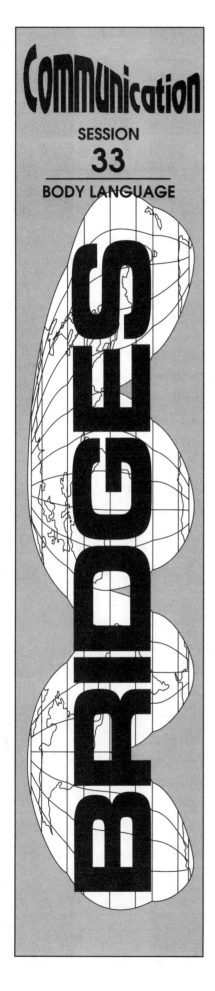

Communication

SESSION
33
BODY LANGUAGE

acilitate a review of the last session dealing with how people sometimes say the opposite of what they're actually thinking. Tell students that in this session they will learn about another way people communicate ... body language.

Body language is the way we communicate through the use of our bodies without using words. In fact, sometimes our bodies may be saying the exact opposite of what our mouths are saying!

For this activity give students an example of body language by folding your arms tightly in front of you. Ask them what that signals to them (anger, unreceptiveness, hostility, etc.). Then tell them that you're happy and see if they believe you. They won't.

Ask students to come to the front to demonstrate other examples. They may use facial expressions as part of body language too.

At the end of the session have students volunteer to show how different kinds of walking styles can indicate diverse moods. They can show happiness, depression, laziness, procrastination, eagerness, apathy, etc., simply by the way they walk. Let their classmates guess how they feel from the way they move.

ADVANCE NOTICE

In the upcoming chapter on Motivation there is a page for students to answer questions regarding a person who has been very successful in spite of handicaps. It would be possible for students to do this page after reading a book or watching a TV show about a handicapped person, but it is suggested that a speaker might be invited so that the students could actually see the person involved and ask him/her questions directly.

Since arrangements will have to be made for this speaker, advance notice is being given.

Hospitals and rehabilitation centers could be good sources for speakers who have overcome great odds. Or contact someone in your business community who has succeeded despite disadvantages, perhaps other than physical ones. Do you know of a business leader in your city who is admired and respected in spite of limitations placed on him/her early in life? Colleges and business clubs may be helpful in locating such a person.

*It is a funny thing
about life;
if you refuse
to accept anything
but the best,
you very often get it.*

Somerset Maugham

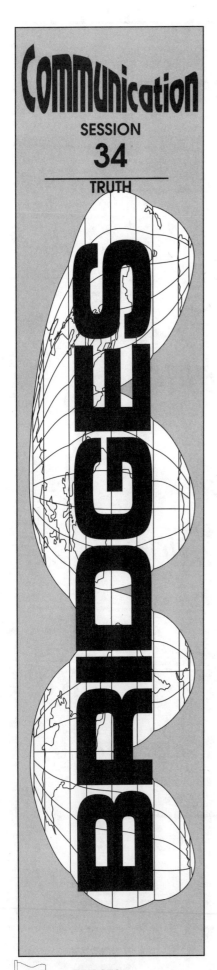

Communication

SESSION
34

TRUTH

efore you begin this activity pass out the letter on the following page or one you have written yourself. This is to be given to students' parents to alert them to the importance of their cooperation in some of the upcoming activities. Tell your students that you would like these taken home, signed and returned in the next few days.

To Tell The Truth

This is a game to play based on the old television show with the same name. Students should try to use everything they've learned about body language and communication.

Divide the class into groups of three players. Let each group go somewhere in the classroom where they will not be overheard as they think of adventures or humorous incidents that have happened to them. After sharing these stories, they all decide on <u>one</u> to use for the game.

One at a time the teacher will call the groups up to the front of the room. The rest of the class will be the audience (or the guessers). They will share their stories when it is their turn.

Each player in the group of three tells his version of the story they selected. The one to whom it really happened must tell the exact, unadorned truth. The other players may embellish as they wish.

The object of the game is to guess who was telling the truth (who the adventure actually happened to) and who was lying. To do this the audience may ask questions of the story teller, trying to "trip him up" and catch him in a lie. The person telling the truth must always do so. If he doesn't know the answer to a question he should say so. He cannot make up an answer, but the other two players may if they wish.

Give the game a certain period of time, perhaps 10 minutes, for the guessers to figure out who was telling the truth. If the storytellers fooled most of the audience, they win!

# Letter To Parents

Dear Parent/Guardian,

As you are probably aware, your child's class is currently involved in a unit on Effective Communication with the **Bridges** program. We will soon be working on a section which deals with listening well and responding to what others say.

The purpose of these activities is to open lines of communication between student and family. The discussion required to answer the questions may be something you already do regularly in your home, or it may be something new. Whatever the case, the idea is that it will cause growth to occur for your child.

The first section asks your child to find out what you would most like to change about him/her. The second part asks that your child answer that same question about members in his/her family. Space is provided for reactions to the suggestions.

I want to assure you that I am not going to look at these pages once they are filled in. Your privacy is absolutely guaranteed. It is simply a method to encourage and facilitate communication within the family. You and your child are free to keep the pages at home.

Please sign and return the form below by _____. Thank you.

If you will be assisting your child with this activity, please have it completed by _____.

Sincerely,

- -

I would be happy to participate in a family discussion with my child for the **Bridges** program and have seen the letter describing its purpose and explanation.

Date _____   Parent/Guardian Signature _____

Destiny
is not a
matter of chance;
it is a
matter of
choice.

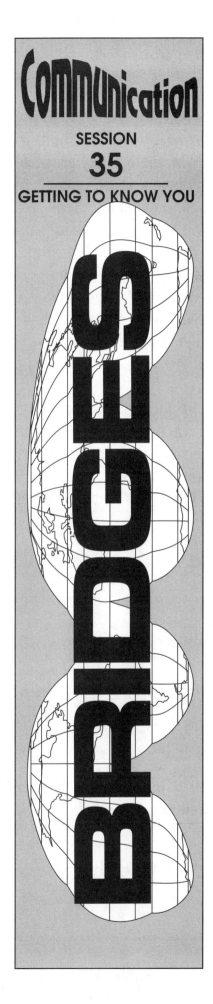

Communication

SESSION
35

GETTING TO KNOW YOU

ntroduce this section by asking students some of the following questions:

How many of you know . . .

• where your father went to elementary school and what it was like for him?

• what kind of living conditions your grandparents had when they were young?

• what was your mother's favorite toy?

• what did your aunts and uncles argue about when they were children?

• when your neighbor was your age, was he/she interested in any sports?

Most children will probably not know the answers to these questions . . . and that's the whole idea!

Pages 126 and 127 will direct students through the interview process with an adult. Go through the questions on those pages in class and see if the students can add any more. Give them a deadline for completing an interview.

Be certain they don't share anything that is considered private because you assured the parents you were going to respect their privacy.

When the interviews are completed, allow some time to share some of the fascinating things they discovered about someone they *thought* they knew very well!

GETTING TO KNOW SOMEONE

Communicating with adults, such as your mom, dad, grandparents, aunts, uncles and neighbors, can be rewarding. They probably lived in a time before you were born, and you can learn a lot from them. They are also special people, and it is to your advantage, as well as theirs, to get to understand them better.

Plan some interview questions to ask an adult you know. Don't ask questions that have one-word answers. Ask questions that require detailed explanations about themselves.

When you do your interview, write the answers next to your questions or tape record the interview if you wish. A tape is something you can pass on to your own children someday. Be certain that you are truly listening to what your interviewee is saying. Be interested! It's more important to hear what they say than to write it down verbatim. You can jot down key words and phrases while you listen or do your writing after the interview is over.

Here are some interview question suggestions:

✓ When were you born?

✓ Where did you live?

✓ What was your house like?

✓ What was your room like?

✓ Did you collect anything? What? Why?

✓ What was your favorite toy? Why? What happened to it?

✓ What did you do in your free time?

✓ Did you have a best friend? Do you know where he/she is today?

✓ Did you have any pets?

✓ What was your favorite book? Where did you get books to read?

✓ What chores did you have to do?

GETTING TO KNOW SOMEONE

✓ Did you have a favorite show or movie?

✓ What kind of music did you like?

✓ What did you want to be when you grew up?

✓ What did you study in school?

✓ What kinds of activities did your school provide?

✓ What were your family traditions?

✓ If you could change one thing in the past, what would it be?

✓ What was important to you as a kid? Is it still important to you now?

✓ How do you think your life is different from what you expected it to be?

✓ Why do you do the work you do?

✓ What is the best thing about your job?

✓ If you could change one thing about your job, what would it be?

Now make up some of your own questions:

_____

_____

_____

_____

_____

_____

_____

_____

_____

Name of person interviewed: _____

Relationship to me: _____

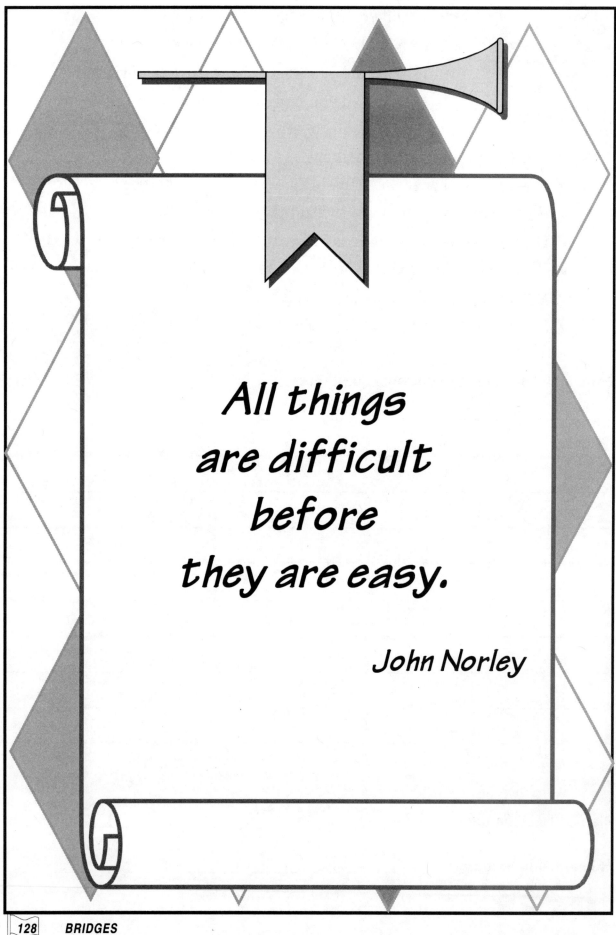

All things
are difficult
before
they are easy.

John Norley

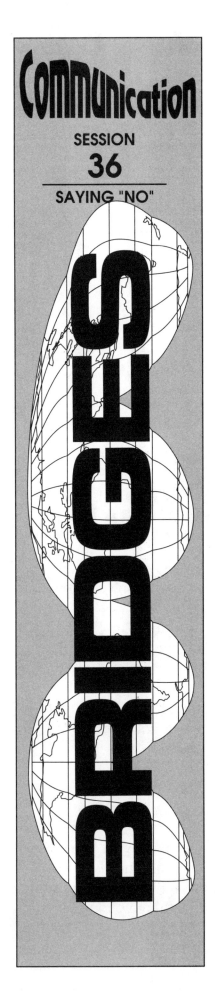

Communication

SESSION
36

SAYING "NO"

his session introduces a technique that students should use to effectively say "No" when they don't want to be involved in something.

Students are given three "rules" to follow:

1. Dismiss the idea, not the person.
2. Continue to say "No;" don't let someone talk you into it.
3. You do not have to give a reason for refusing to do something.

After the class has read page 130 together and discussed the technique, they may want to do some role playing. Suggestions include saying "No" to:

- Drugs
- Smoking
- R-rated movies
- Shoplifting
- Being someplace they shouldn't be
- Staying out after curfew

After each role playing situation, discuss the results with the students.

NO. No! No! No! No! NO! No! NO.

Have you ever been in a situation where you know that you want to say "No," but it's very hard to do so? Perhaps you're afraid that the other kids will call you a sissy. Or maybe you think that everyone's doing it, and you don't want to be left out of the crowd. There's a chance that you just want to make an impression.

Whatever the reason, you're going to find that as you get older there are an increasing number of temptations you'll face — and want to turn down. How can you go about saying "No" to good friends or to people you'd like to have as friends?

First of all, remember:

TURN DOWN THE ACTIVITY, BUT DON'T REJECT THE PERSON.

Let's see how this works. Suppose someone tells you to come over to her house after school. Her parents won't be home so you can do all sorts of "neat" things that you couldn't normally do. In this situation you have several choices.
- You can go to her house, even though you don't really want to.
- You can tell her no, but you're afraid she will get upset with you.

But there is another, better solution for you. Try saying something like, "Hey, you know I always like to be with you. You're a lot of fun. However, I really can't go to your house when your parents aren't home. But how about this? I got a new video game, and you could come over to my house! Let's do that, O.K?"

Notice that if you take this approach you are not going to be involved in something you shouldn't, and you're neither offending the person nor missing out on some fun!

Let's suppose that the person doesn't go along with your suggestion. What then? Well, you should continue saying "No" until she recognizes that you really mean it. Keep making other suggestions, but don't give in if it's something you know you shouldn't do. And you don't have to give a reason for refusing to do something you know is wrong. This is your life, and you don't want to mess it up for someone else. What kind of friend would insist that you should, anyway? Think about it.

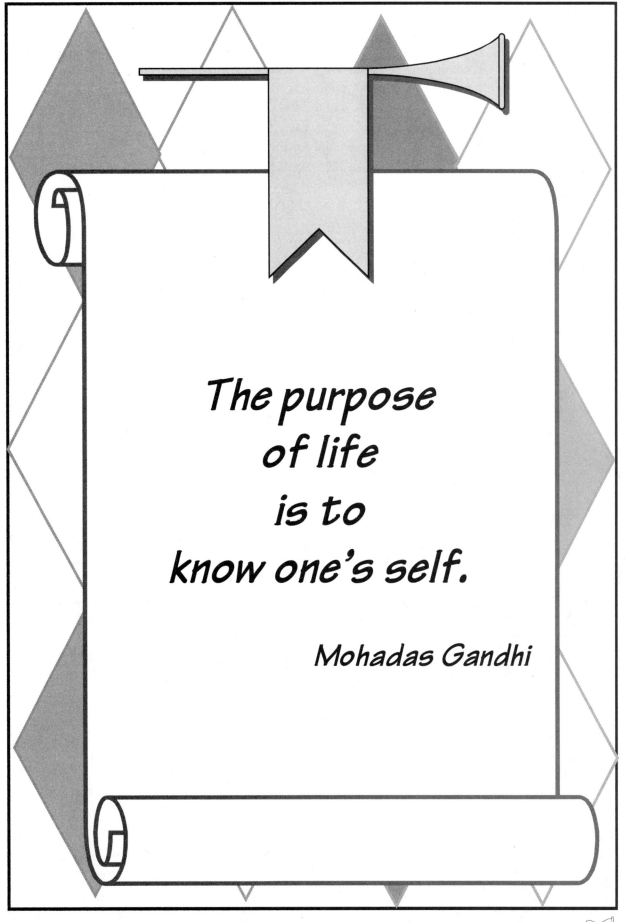

*The purpose
of life
is to
know one's self.*

Mohadas Gandhi

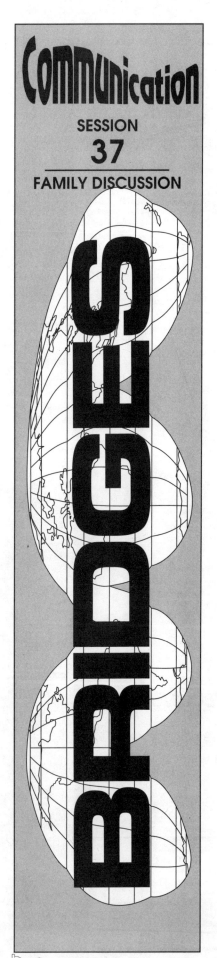

Communication

BRIDGES

y now your students should have returned their Letter to Parents indicating parental cooperation with the students on a family discussion. Now it is time to complete the discussion.

Copy and pass out the following four pages to each student. Review the procedure and assure the students that the answers are for *their own use* and will *not* be discussed in class. The purpose is to open a meaningful dialogue between student and family members in order to increase the effectiveness of communication within the family.

Set a date when the questionnaires should be completed so that students can really plan and carry out the interviews needed with their family members.

MY FAMILY DISCUSSES ME

Name

Ask the members of your family these questions. Be sure to listen with respect when they give their answers and write their responses down. Don't argue! Let them know that their opinion is important to you. Be certain that you write the exact meaning of what they say!

1. If you could change just one thing about me, what would it be?

    _____

    _____

    _____

2. Why would you want this change?

    _____

    _____

    _____

When you get the answers to these questions, take time to think through what has been said, then write down how you feel about it.

_____

_____

_____

FAMILY DISCUSSION continued

Now tell your family how you feel about what they said. Afterwards, ask yourself if you were able to express your real feelings. Can change occur? Write down how you will try.

_____

_____

_____

Now set a time to communicate on the progress of your change. It may be a few days from now or a few weeks.

Date to meet again and talk: _____

After this meeting write down how your family feels you are doing now and tell how you feel about it.

_____

_____

_____

Now make a list of the things your family really LIKES about you!

_____

_____

_____

COMMUNICATING WITH MY FAMILY

If you could change one thing about each person in your household, what would it be? Then record how family members feel about this.

1. Person _____

   Change _____

   Reaction _____

   _____

2. Person _____

   Change _____

   Reaction _____

   _____

3. Person _____

   Change _____

   Reaction _____

   _____

4. Person _____

   Change _____

   Reaction _____

   _____

COMMUNICATING WITH
MY FAMILY continued

Is the person willing to make the change? How will change occur?

1. Person _____
   How _____
   Date to meet again _____
   Evaluation _____

2. Person _____
   How _____
   Date to meet again _____
   Evaluation _____

3. Person _____
   How _____
   Date to meet again _____
   Evaluation _____

4. Person _____
   How _____
   Date to meet again _____
   Evaluation _____

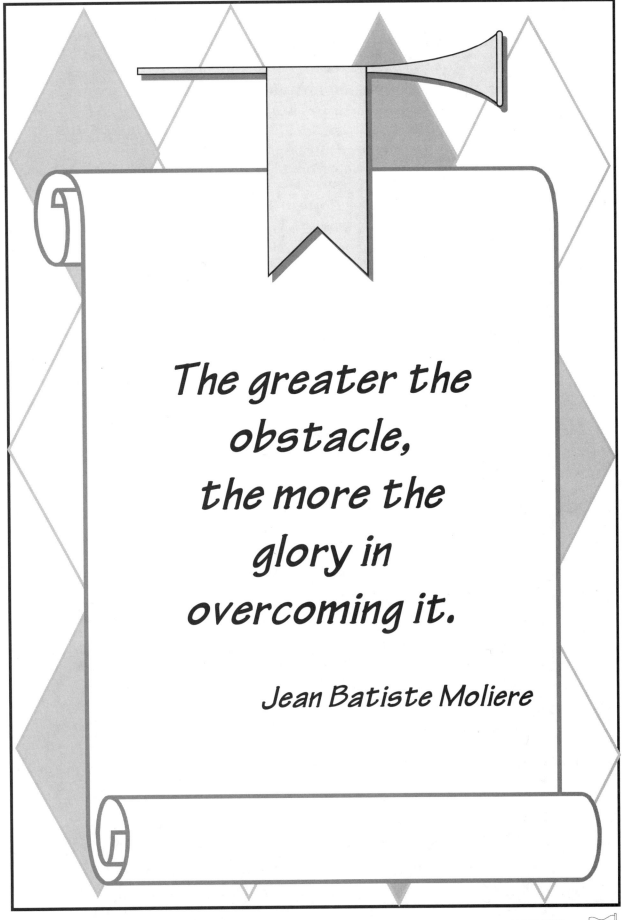

The greater the
obstacle,
the more the
glory in
overcoming it.

Jean Batiste Moliere

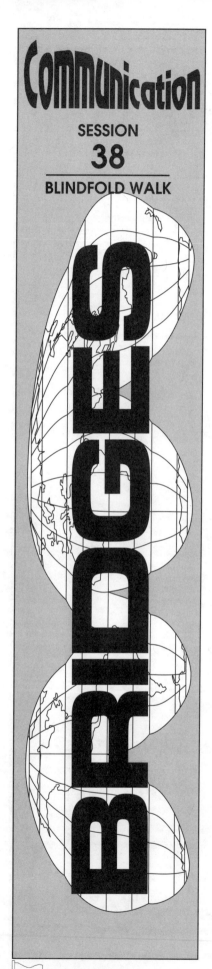

Communication

SESSION
38

BLINDFOLD WALK

his game is designed to help students learn that what they say can really make a difference! They must say exactly what they mean.

Blindfold Walk

(This game could be done in a gym using ropes and cones, etc., or in a classroom using chairs and desks. The open space of a gym will be easier. Perhaps try both!)

Match students with a partner prior to a time when the whole class will be leaving the classroom for a while, like before recess. Then, while they are gone, rearrange the desks and place obstacles in the room to make it difficult, but not impossible, to get around. Bells or other noisy items are good obstacles. Make sure, though, that there is a definite path that can be followed but that it is different than your usual classroom setup.

Before the students enter the classroom they are to gather close by, where they cannot see the new setup. Blindfold one of a pair of students previously matched. Only one pair of students will go at a time, while the other students stand on the perimeter of the room to observe and learn. The blindfolded student must follow his partner's verbal instructions as to how to go down the path without touching any obstacles. No one can touch the blindfolded student to lead him, and he is not to use his hands to feel his way through the course.

When one partnership is finished, another volunteers to leave the room and those observing will then rearrange the room anew. You may choose to time the pairs to see how they compare.

Note: *Follow-up discussion should include what communication techniques made it easier or more difficult to walk the course. Stress the role of active listening.*

Variation: *The Trust Walk is a version of this game in which communication is all non-verbal. One partner leads the other through the course using the sense of touch only.*

One's mind,
once stretched
by a new idea,
never regains
its original
dimensions.

Oliver Wendell Holmes

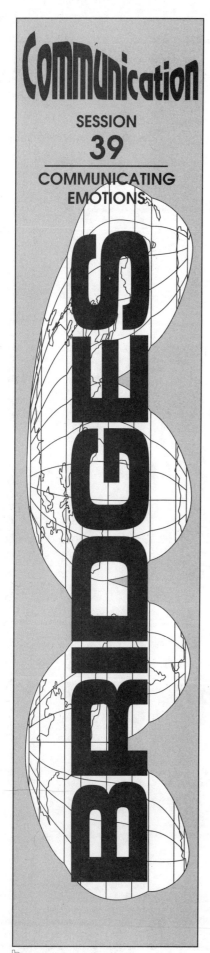

et out the list of emotions the class brainstormed in the previous chapter on Sensitivity. If you no longer have it, make a new list. Write all the emotions you can think of on separate pieces of paper to make one deck of cards.

Now have the class brainstorm all the forms of communication they can think of and write them on separate pieces of a different colored paper to form a second deck.

Put the two decks of cards side by side. Have students draw a card from each deck. They must then use the form of communication they drew to show the emotion they drew. For example, if a student chooses "song" for the form of communication and "sad" for the emotion, he/she may either make up a song that shows sadness or sing a familiar song which demonstrates the emotion.

The quality of a person's life is in direct proportion to their commitment to excellence, regardless of their chosen field of endeavor.

Vincent T. Lombardi

Any thoughts?
Put them here!

The greatest
calamity is
not to have failed,
but to have
failed to try.

Anonymous

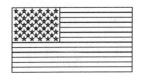

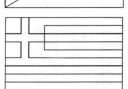

Motivation

Helping students understand

the meaning and importance

of setting and achieving

goals

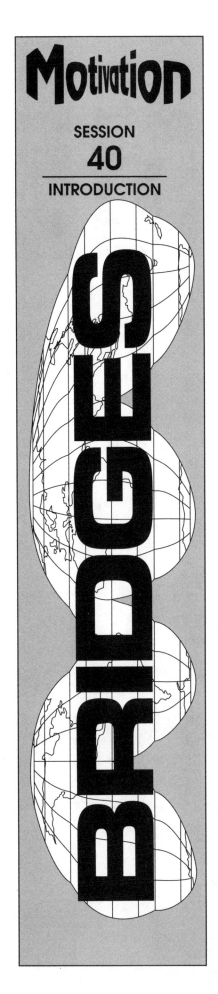

Motivation

SESSION 40

INTRODUCTION

ead the following page on motivation with your class as an introduction to this session. Ask students to think of examples of people they know or have heard about who were really motivated. Let them give examples in their own lives where motivation has made a big difference. Be sure they recognize that different people are motivated by different things.

Talk about *optimism* and its part in accomplishing goals. Remind students of the saying you discussed in the chapter on self-esteem:

**If you think you can,
or
if you think you can't,
you're right!**

Optimism is the fuel that keeps the engine of our motivation running! If we do not believe in ourselves, we won't accomplish much. So simple — so true.

After you have discussed motivation, compare it to anxiety. Anxiety is a nervousness about accomplishing something. Students may feel motivated *and* anxious before a big test or a skills contest. However, it's the motivation that makes them do their best and the anxiety that might get in the way. The trick is to be so well prepared, confident and optimistic that anxiety is kept out of the picture as much as possible.

At the end of the session, be sure that students understand the meaning of "goals." Ask them to start thinking of goals they would like to accomplish. You do not need to be any more specific than this because you will be going into more detail later.

Note: *Although children have no doubt experienced negative motivation in their lives, we will not be touching on this in this chapter. We prefer to keep it positive!*

Motivation

 Have you ever found that you were able to do something that at one time you thought would be impossible?

 Have you ever read about someone who seems to be superhuman because he/she can accomplish so much?

Each year the Special Olympics are held there are stories about how athletes have overcome great odds in order to compete. We read about these people and try to imagine what it must be like to be so dedicated. These athletes are terrific examples of what motivation can do!

We've all experienced motivation in our own lives too. Perhaps it came when our team worked extra hard to win a game. Or it might have been when we studied especially diligently for a test. Maybe we had to earn some extra money in order to buy something we really wanted. Whatever caused it, our motivation certainly was a factor in making us work harder than we would have done otherwise.

☞ **Have you ever learned to do something simply by practicing it over and over?**

☞ **Have you noticed how the people who seem to get what they want in life are the ones who set goals for themselves?**

You will find that your life is much happier if you are motivated to accomplish your goals. That's what this chapter is all about!

Hitch
your wagon
to a star!

Ralph Waldo Emerson

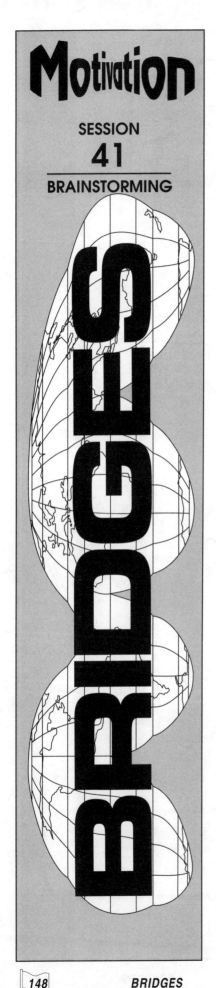

Motivation

SESSION
41

BRAINSTORMING

During the last class session you asked the students to start thinking of some goals they would like to accomplish. Ask them to turn to their page entitled "Brainstorming," and read the text together.

As they can see, they'll now be writing all the goals they can think of in 10 minutes on their Brainstorming page. They should continue writing for the entire 10 minutes without stopping. As the teacher, you can make this seem like a fun challenge to them! It doesn't matter what the goals are, just as long as they represent something *they* want to accomplish.

Reassure the class before they begin writing that this is simply a brainstorming session . . . they will not be required to accomplish all the goals they write down!

Save these lists of goals as students will be working with them in the next session.

IMPORTANT NOTE:
Session 43 (the session after the next) is the one we gave you advance notice to invite a speaker to the class. We hope you have made the proper arrangements!

Brainstorming!

Brainstorming!

When you brainstorm ideas, you write them down as fast as you can! You don't do any kind of evaluation until later.

Right now you're going to brainstorm all the possible goals you can think of for yourself. Have you ever thought you'd like to be able to stand on your head? . . . learn to cook spaghetti? . . . get your chores done before anyone reminds you about them? . . . learn to type? . . . take drawing lessons? . . . introduce yourself to a shy person? . . . learn how to whistle? . . . stop biting your nails?

Write down whatever goals you can think of on the numbered lines here. Flip the paper over and use the back if you need to. Don't stop writing until your teachers tells you to do so. You'll be given 10 minutes.

1. _____
2. _____
3. _____
4. _____
5. _____
6. _____
7. _____
8. _____
9. _____
10. _____
11. _____
12. _____
13. _____
14. _____
15. _____

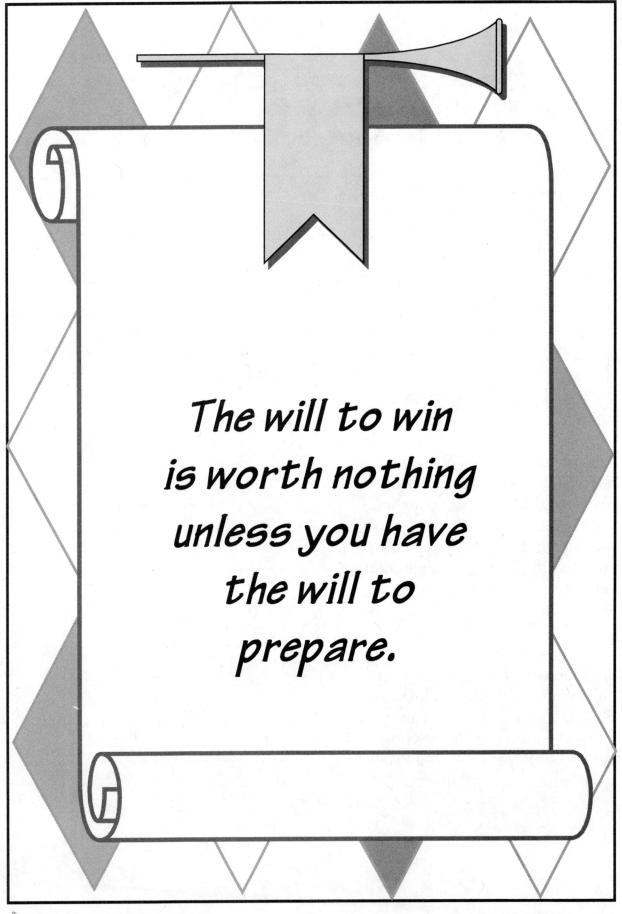

The will to win
is worth nothing
unless you have
the will to
prepare.

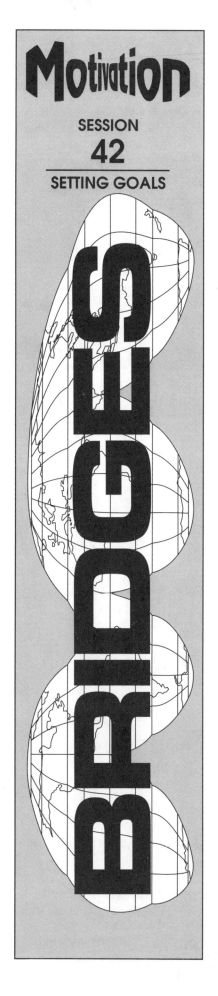

Motivation

his session gets into the specifics about setting and accomplishing goals. The student pages (152-154) do not need to be discussed in great detail, but should be read by the students.

One of the most important steps in goal setting is the process of visualizing it. Discuss this in detail with the class because they are probably not familiar with the term "visualize." Tell them that they should be in a quiet, relaxed setting where their mind forms a picture of themselves accomplishing the goal. Their feelings of success should seem absolutely real.

At the end of the session, direct the class back to their list of brainstormed goals (page 149). Have them cross out any which are not realistic or cannot be measured.

SETTING & ACCOMPLISHING GOALS

Let's talk a little bit about setting goals and then accomplishing them. Here's a plan for you to use:

- **Make the goal realistic.**

- **Divide large goals into small steps.**

- **Make the goal something you can measure.**

- **Set a date for completion.**

- **Record how well you are doing in reaching the goal.**

- **Visualize yourself accomplishing the goal.**

- **Recognize that there may be setbacks, but don't give up!**

- **Keep on trying. Remember, if you have set a realistic goal, then it is achievable!**

If you are serious about your goals, you will soon see that these steps will make it easier for you to accomplish them. This plan is very specific. If you follow these steps, you won't fall into the trap of just having a vague idea that someday, somehow, you're going to do something. You'll <u>know</u> you're going to succeed!

READ ON FOR MORE DETAILS ABOUT FOLLOWING THESE STEPS!

REALISTIC GOALS are goals that you will be able to accomplish. They may take a lot of work, but you will be able to succeed. For example, it is not realistic to set your goal to skip grades 7 - 12 and go directly to college. But it may be realistic to decide that you will maintain a B+ average for the school year.

Let's look at how that realistic goal can be accomplished using the steps from the previous page.

1. **DIVIDE THE GOAL** into small steps so that you can easily see the progress you are making. This will make you feel great, too, because you'll know you're on your way to something big! For example, you might have smaller goals such as:
- I will study each night for at least 1 hour.
- I will complete all assignments on time.
- I will start long-term projects when assigned and work on them each day until they are done.
- If I don't understand something, I will get help immediately.
- I will check over all my work after it is done.
- I will study as soon as I know a test is coming by practicing sample questions.
- If my grade falls below a B+ in any subject, I will ask the teacher for extra credit work so I can bring the grade up.

2. Each of the small steps above can be **MEASURED**. You can actually see that you are doing what you said you would do. There's nothing vague about them. (It would be hard to measure a goal such as "I will be nicer to my sister," but you could measure a goal like "I will play with my sister for 15 minutes a day.")

SETTING & ACCOMPLISHING GOALS

3. **SET A DATE** for the completion of the goal. A goal that only exists as an idea will not get you anywhere, but one with a date attached to it will assure progress. In this example, when you get in the habit of completing all your homework every night, you know you won't have any late papers.

4. **THE RECORDS** you keep of your progress will help you see how well you are doing. When you want to maintain the B+ average you should make a chart with all your small goal steps on it. Check off each day that you accomplish the goals. Then keep a separate record of your grades so that you'll know you've got the high marks you've been aiming for.

5. **VISUALIZING** yourself accomplishing your goal is very important. It helps maintain that positive attitude you need. Picture yourself having your homework done early each evening and going to school prepared the next day. Picture yourself having your long-term projects done with time to spare! Picture yourself opening up your report card and feeling terrific! Get those feelings of accomplishment in your mind so that you KNOW they're worth working toward.

6. **SETBACKS** are natural occurrences on your way to achieving your goal, but that is no reason to quit. One poor grade on daily work doesn't mean that you won't get that B+. It just means that you will work even harder on the next assignment. And you will find it much more satisfying when you have succeeded despite the setbacks!

TO DO: Look back at your list of brainstormed goals now. Cross out any that are not realistic or can't be measured.

You Can Do It!

All it takes is determination and your goal plan!

*The pessimist
sees the difficulty
in every
opportunity;
the optimist
sees the opportunity
in every difficulty.*

L.P. Jacks

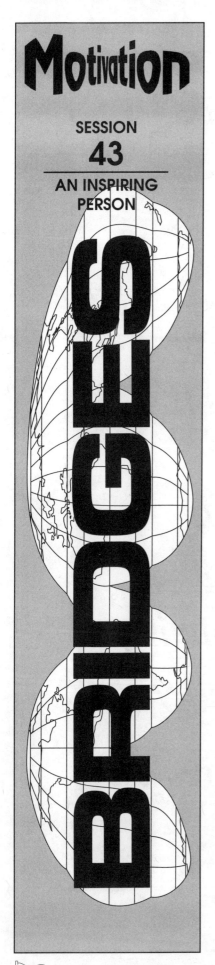

Motivation

SESSION
43

AN INSPIRING PERSON

his session deals with overcoming great odds. It is hoped that you have found a speaker who has overcome an adversity to visit your class.

Before your speaker arrives, ask him how he would like to be introduced to the class. It's possible that he would like for you to tell about his current accomplishments yourself, then open it up for class discussion and questions. Be sure he knows that the class is studying motivation and goal setting so that the talk can be geared toward these subjects.

Go over the questions on the next pages (157-158) with the class to familiarize them with what they will be listening for and asking about. Then have students put their books away and give the speaker their full attention. This will give them a setting for productive listening without the distraction of books.

Allow for question and answer time at the end of the talk.

NOTE: *If you were unable to get a speaker to come in, perhaps you could read a book or story to the class (or students could read on their own) about Jesse Owens, Helen Keller, Albert Einstein or Franklin Roosevelt for example. There are many other inspiring people about whom much has been written.*

After the book/story is finished they should fill in pages 157 and 158.

INSPIRATION

Name of person _____

What did this person accomplish? _____
_____

Did he/she set any goals? If so, what were they? _____
_____
_____

What obstacle(s) did he/she have to overcome? _____
_____
_____
_____

How did he/she overcome the obstacles?_____
_____
_____
_____
_____
_____

INSPIRATION

continued

What qualities do you admire most about this person? _____
_____
_____
_____
_____
_____

Does this person motivate you to try something? If so, what is it?
_____
_____
_____
_____
_____

Progress always involves risk; you can't steal second base and keep your foot on first.

Frederick Wilcox

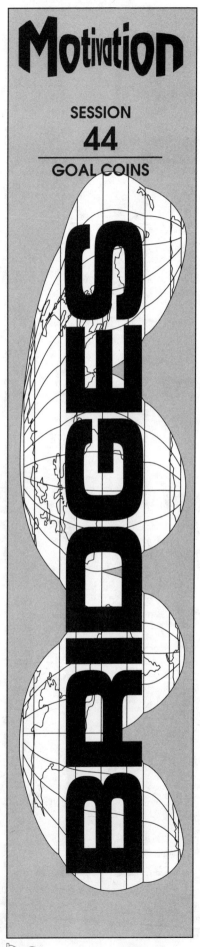

his session is a combination game, bulletin board, and goal setting activity.

To begin, copy and pass out the student page with the "goal coins." (They're called goal coins as a play on words . . . gold coins.) Ask students to think of a goal they can accomplish within a month and write it on the coin, making sure no one else sees it. They should only tell you their goal and you should write it on a duplicate coin for display on the classroom bulletin board. This will prevent students from recognizing one another's handwriting and keep their identity a secret.

Read the goals to the class and place your "coins" on the bulletin board.

For the next month students are to watch their classmates carefully and try to guess which person set which goal. Be sure to follow up on this to discover who met their goals and who guessed which classmates had met which goals. You could turn it into a challenge to see who has the most correct guesses.

Whose GOALS ARE Whose?

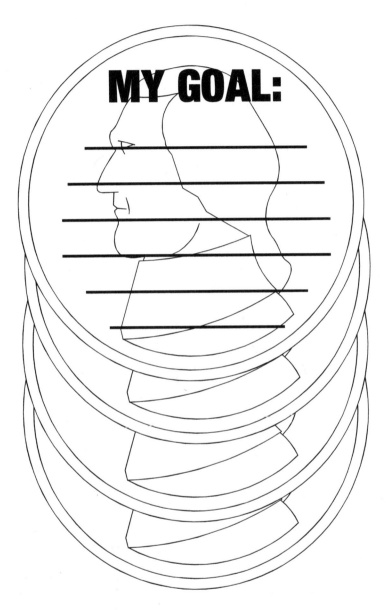

MY GOAL:

_____

_____

_____

_____

_____

_____

Think of a goal that you want to work on for the next month. Write your goal on this coin, but make sure no one else sees it.

See how well you can do at accomplishing your own goal, and try to determine what your classmates' goals were and which ones each belongs to.

Your classmates should be able to notice how you are doing with your goal, and you will probably notice your class-mates doing certain things to accomplish their goals too. But don't tell anyone what yours is. See if they can figure it out!

Your teacher will be writing everyone's goals on a duplicate coin in his/her own handwrit-ing for display. This will pre-vent students from recognizing each other's handwriting.

If you wait for tomorrow, tomorrow comes. If you don't wait for tomorrow, tomorrow comes.

Sierra Leone

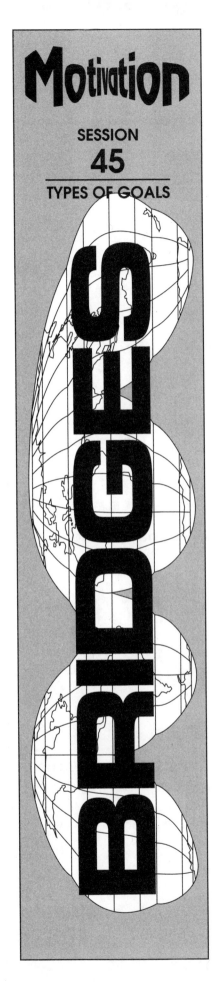

Motivation

SESSION
45

TYPES OF GOALS

his session deals with short-, medium- and long-range goals. Have the students read the following pages about these different types of goals. Be sure to mention how the examples on the page fit the standards made for setting goals in the previous lessons, especially in terms of being realistic and measurable.

When you've finished discussing the types of goals, have students complete the next pages on categorizing the goals they brainstormed on page 149.

The 3 Types of Goals

Short-Term Goals

Short-term goals are those that can be accomplished in a very short time. Examples include

- I will do the dishes immediately after dinner
- I will practice the piano for 30 minutes each day
- I will clean my room at least once a week
- I will visit my neighbor at least twice a week

With short-term goals, you know right away how you're doing. You can see results within a day, week or month.

Medium-Term Goals

Medium-term goals take longer than short-term goals. You have to work more consistently at them. Examples include

- I will learn how to type
- I will take a course in self defense
- I will learn how to do at least 3 kinds of dives

You will see progress in medium-term goals, of course, but they won't actually be accomplished in less than a month. They may take a year or longer!

Long-Term Goals

Long-term goals are those you set your sights on for the distant future. They may take as long as 5 years to achieve or even longer. That's why we divide them into small steps! Examples include

- I will get accepted into the Air Force Academy as a student
- I will become captain of the gymnastics team
- I will get my degree in teaching
- I will learn to speak Spanish fluently

These goals take a lot of long, sustained effort, but there are rewards as you go. Think how great you'll feel when you accomplish them!

Your Goals

Now it's time for you to be categorizing the goals you made in your brainstorming session earlier. You should have already crossed out those that were not realistic or not measurable. Now go through the list again. Write "S", "M", or "L" beside each goal indicating whether they are Short-Term, Medium-Term, or Long-Term Goals. Then transfer the goals to these charts.

Short-Term Goals

	Target Date	Date Completed

Your Goals (continued)

Medium-Term Goals	Target Date	Date Completed

Long-Term Goals	Target Date	Date Completed

If you never reach, you're never going to grab what you're after.

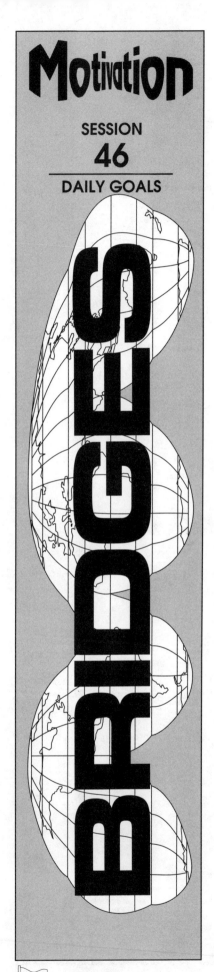

Motivation

SESSION
46
DAILY GOALS

ince students this age frequently cannot keep focused on goals far in the future, this activity is designed to help them on a day-by-day basis.

At the beginning of the day, pass out the Goals Chart to each student (following page). They should fill out a goal they are going to work on that day, making sure it is realistic and attainable. The goal may be part of a long-term objective, or it may simply be something they want to try for the day. These are private papers and do not have to be shared with anyone else.

At the end of the day, provide a short period of time for students to note in the "Evaluation" sections on their chart how well they did at accomplishing each goal.

This activity should be repeated for the rest of the school week. If a student wishes to work on the same goal for more than one day, that is perfectly acceptable. In fact, unless it is a goal that is very easily accomplished, it would be a good idea to repeat it over a longer period of time than just one day.

If you decide to continue with this activity after the end of the week, students should be encouraged to keep the papers so they can look back to see if they have made progress in learning how to set and accomplish their goals.

GOALS CHART

Name _____ Week of _____

Goal	Evaluation
Goal	Evaluation
Goal	Evaluation
Goal	Evaluation
Goal	Evaluation

If you can do it on purpose, it won't happen by accident.

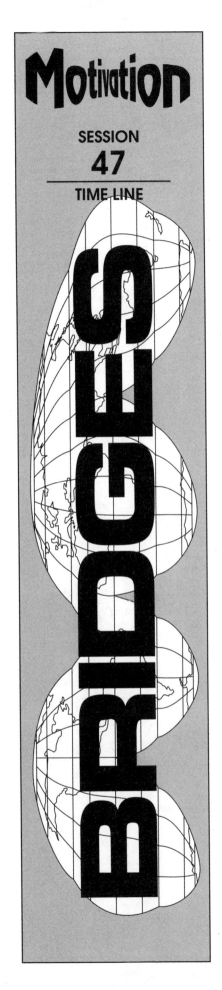

Motivation

SESSION
47

TIME LINE

his activity gives students a concrete, visual way in which to see how well they are succeeding in reaching their goals. It also gives them a chance to display to their peers what they have accomplished so far in the school year.

Procedure

Give each student a long (36" to 48"), narrow (3" to 5") piece of paper on which they should draw a time line of the school year. Using colorful markers or crayons, students should use symbols to indicate the successes they have been proud of thus far. These may be in-school or out-of-school activities. For future dates they should show what they would like to accomplish. As the year progresses they may indicate on the timeline when they succeed in meeting each of their goals.

Students may draw time lines from their birth until the present time, showing positive events in their lives. Then they should indicate long-term goals for the future. Intermediate goals on the way toward the long-term goals should also be indicated. For example, good grades in high school would be necessary to a long term goal of getting into college, and a college education would be mandatory for becoming a lawyer, etc.

Symbols used on the time line should be simple so that the focus is on the goals, not on the artwork.

The time lines may be displayed in the classroom, compiled in a class booklet or kept by the students. Students will also enjoy some time to share their time line with others.

A variation on the time line would be a student journal describing a day in their life now, then a page indicating what they think a day will be like in 10, 15 or 20 years. They may also like to draw a picture of themselves as they think they will look years from now.

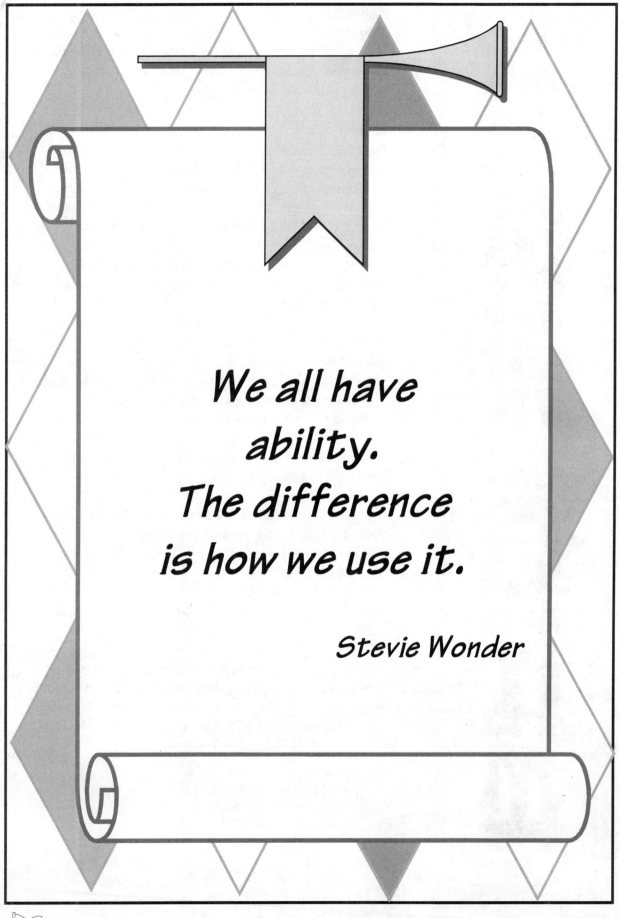

*We all have
ability.
The difference
is how we use it.*

Stevie Wonder

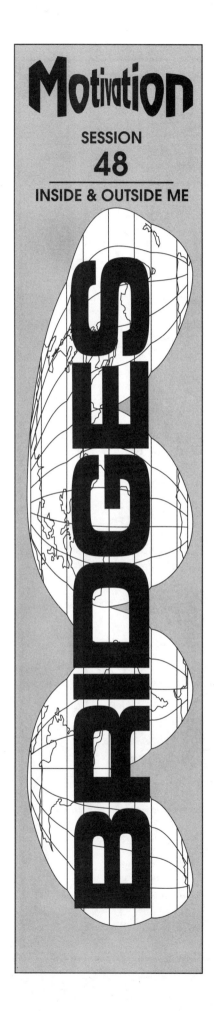

his activity is designed to help students recognize their uniqueness and to demonstrate in a concrete way how well they are meeting their goals.

Procedure

Students should bring a shoebox to class. They should decorate the outside in a manner representative of their outside appearance. They may use photographs, drawings or symbols.

On the inside of the box students will place objects or pictures that stand for some of their good qualities; for example, a picture of a dog could mean that they care for animals. There is no upward limit regarding the number of qualities they may represent, so they should be encouraged to think of as many as possible.

In addition, students should place at least one symbol in the box that represents a self-improvement goal. If they are inclined to procrastinate, they might want to put a calendar in the box to represent the "tomorrows" they don't want to wait for to do something. Each day they make progress toward their goal, they should open the box and tear off a little bit of that symbol. When the symbol is gone, the goal should be completed!

A positive quality symbol should be placed in the box to replace the self-improvement goal above as an indication that it exists. In the example above, the former procrastinator may want to put a list of the work he/she got done "on time" in the box.

If desired, a new goal symbol may be introduced to make this an ongoing activity. By doing this, each student will always have a particular goal he/she is trying to accomplish.

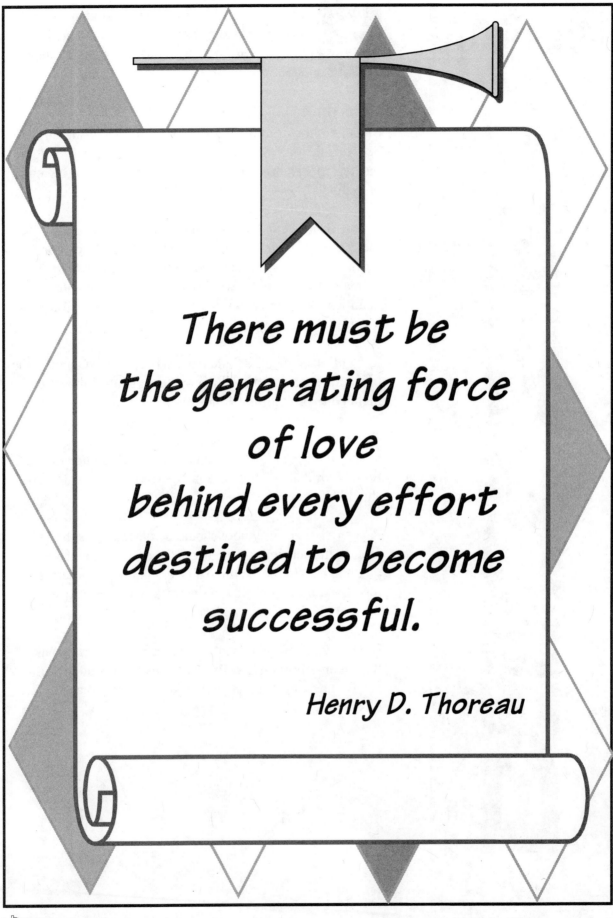

There must be
the generating force
of love
behind every effort
destined to become
successful.

Henry D. Thoreau

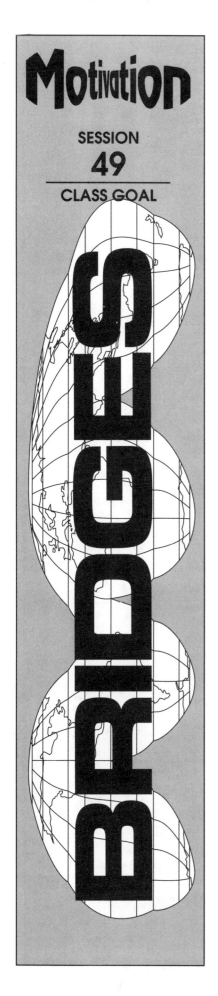

Motivation

SESSION
49
CLASS GOAL

BRIDGES

This activity is designed to bring the class together in setting a group goal.

Begin by discussing any "ground rules" you wish to set before the class has a brainstorming session about what the goal will be. The rules could include

1) Every person in class must be able to participate;
2) The class must be able to accomplish it within a determined time frame and with a determined amount of out-of-class time;
3) It must be something that benefits someone outside the classroom;
4) It must be approved by the teacher and the principal.

Then brainstorm for ideas. Open a discussion about the class goal and list all ideas. For example, community service projects and fundraisers for a worthy cause are both good goals for a class to set.

Evaluate the ideas according to the class criteria, and then determine which one is best. Obviously, the goal your students choose can be as complicated or uncomplicated as you wish. YOU set the standards you'll be comfortable with.

Most importantly, DO IT!

Small
opportunities
are often
the beginning
of great
enterprises.

Demosthenes

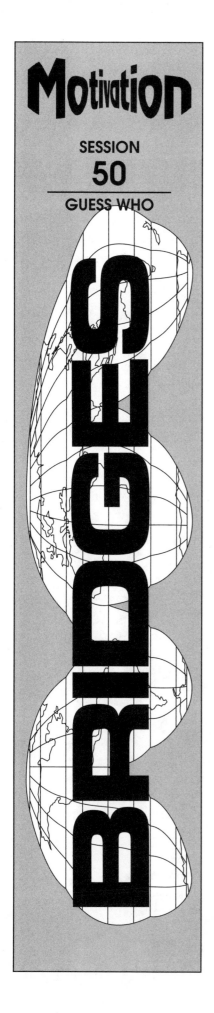

Motivation

BRIDGES

his game, and each of its variations, is designed to help students learn how to communicate with each other in a positive manner, hear positive qualities of others and build confidence in themselves. It is a good game to end the **Bridges** program for the year.

Procedure

Send one or more students out of the room. Have the remaining students identify a classmate as the "Mystery Person." When the other students return to the room they are to ask POSITIVE questions to try to find out who the "Mystery Person" is. They may ask a question then call on anyone in the class to respond. If that person doesn't know the answer he/she should say so. Then someone else can be asked the question. The "winner" is the person who first guesses the identify of the "Mystery Person."

Be sure that, before you begin the game, students know why they are playing the game! Discuss the benefits of positive questions and responses and give examples of questions that can be answered yes or no without hurting anyone's feelings. Some good questions might be: "Does this person play football?" and "Does this person have red hair?" Also give examples of questions that may not necessarily be answered with a "yes" or "no," but which will help identify the person, like "What is this person's favorite subject in school?" and "How many pets does this person have?"

Then give examples of the kinds of questions not to ask: those that might hurt someone's feelings. Help students recognize how to avoid asking these questions. Poor questions to ask would be: "Does this person get poor grades?" and "Does this person get in trouble a lot?" Be sure students understand that a negative answer to a positive questions can also be hurtful and to avoid these, "Does this person get good grades?" with an answer of "No."

Variation: Students could stand in a circle around a blindfolded classmate. The student in the center turns around several times and then stops, pointing at a classmate in the circle. He/She then asks positive questions of the group about the "Mystery Person" to determine who he/she is.

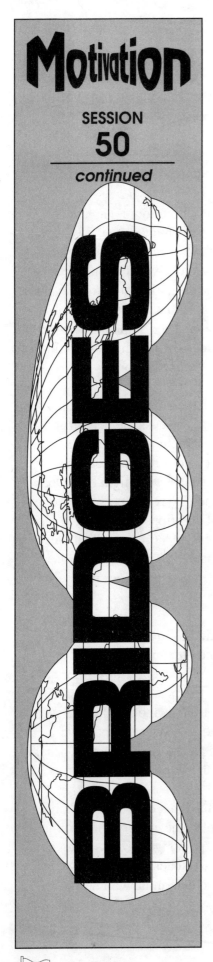

Motivation

SESSION
50
continued

BRIDGES

The group can answer together or one at a time. If the "Mystery Person" answers the questions he/she can disguise his/her voice.

If the "Mystery Person" is difficult for others to identify, the teacher may offer some positive comments about him/her to assist the blindfolded student.

Another way to facilitate this game would be for each student, prior to the game, to write some accomplishments and positive qualities about himself/herself and let the teacher hold these to use if necessary.

Variation: The teacher can make handouts giving positive clues about everyone in the class. The students then try to identify as many of their classmates as possible.

Don't bother about
genius.
Don't worry about
being clever.
Place your trust
in hard work,
perseverance
and determination.

Sir Frederic Treves

Obstacles
are those
frightful things
you see when
you take your eyes
off your goals.

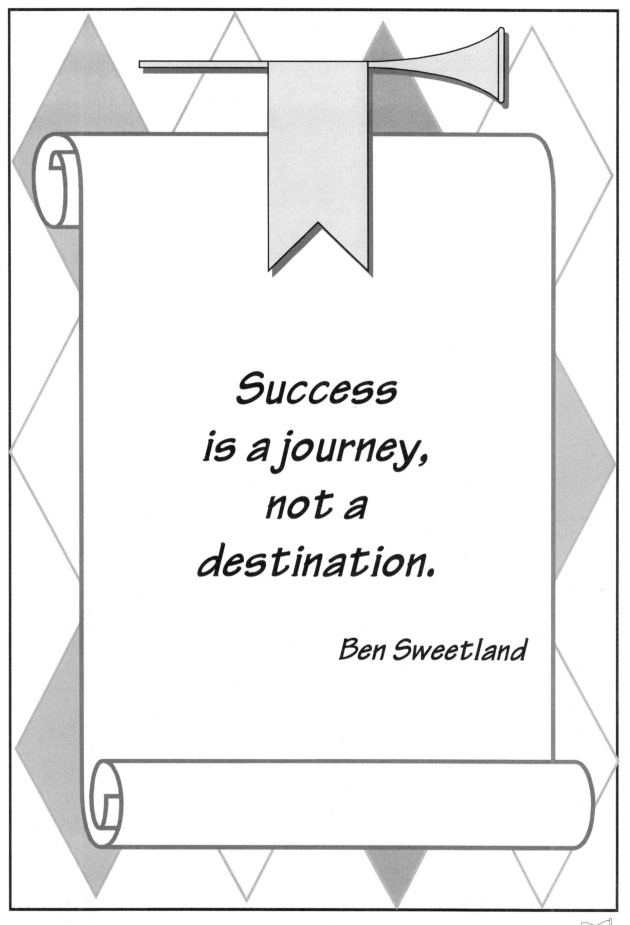

Success
is a journey,
not a
destination.

Ben Sweetland

Any thoughts?
Put them here!

_____
_____
_____
_____
_____
_____
_____
_____
_____
_____
_____
_____
_____
_____
_____
_____
_____
_____